# HISTORIC
# LAKEVIEW
# CEMETERY
*of Cheyenne*

# HISTORIC
# LAKEVIEW
# CEMETERY
## *of Cheyenne*

STARLEY TALBOTT & MICHAEL E. KASSEL

*Foreword by Sharon Lass Field*

THE
History
PRESS

Published by The History Press
Charleston, SC
www.historypress.com

*Front cover, top left*: The only mausoleum in Lakeview, dedicated to the Bradley family; *top right*: Joseph Stimson; *center left*: Nellie Tayloe Ross; *bottom*: The burial of Mrs. Kono at Lakeview.

First published 2023

Manufactured in the United States

ISBN 978-1-54025-767-3

Library of Congress Control Number: 2023934797

# CONTENTS

# FOREWORD

If you want to put a person's life together, for whatever reason, the first question to ask is, "Where are they buried?" In my opinion, a cemetery is not just a place of sorrow but a final place of rest that gives a future relative or researcher the opportunity to let the deceased tell their story—and everyone has a story to tell.

The records that may be available at an individual's time of death are invaluable sources we can use to find the pieces to put together a family or an individual puzzle. A cemetery is also a place for contemplating, looking back on memories, bird watching or just going for a restful walk. The landscaping, flora and fauna make it such a special environment for this task. The word went out from our city fathers many years ago to "plant trees wherever you can find a place to plant them," so we have the lovely trees in our downtown and cemeteries to enjoy today.

This foreword will try to put together the history of Lakeview Cemetery in the hopes that you will appreciate all the years of hard work and effort our city has been through to ensure we have this beautiful resting place for our families and friends. History allows you to put your search in the correct period and allows you, the researcher, to understand some of the decisions and events experienced by the object of your investigation to explain what, when and how they lived. After you read this book, do take the time to take a walk through our Lakeview Cemetery to appreciate the lovely grounds that are so lovingly kept for all of us here today to understand a bit of the past.

In the spring of 1867, General Grenville Dodge reported in his book *How We Built the Union Pacific Railway*, "While we were camped here (the division point on Crow Creek where Cheyenne now stands), the Indians swooped down out of the ravine of Crow Creek and attacked a Mormon grading train and outfit that was coming from Salt Lake to take work on the road and killed two of its men. Our cavalry hastily mounted and drove off the Indians and saved their stock. We buried the men and started the graveyard of the future city, now the capitol of Wyoming." General Dodge neglected to report exactly where these two men were buried, and sadly, the first burial sites in Cheyenne have been lost to history.

When the first train chugged into Cheyenne on November 13, 1867, and the first passenger train arrived from the East Coast the next day, the scene to greet them consisted of a few tents and hastily constructed buildings. Fort D.A. Russell, named in memory of Major General David Allen Russell, had been established about one mile west. To welcome the train, railroad workers mingled with the military and railroad "followers" looking for "opportunity" from the devastation of the East Coast and South during the Civil War. There were certainly no official buildings or offices to establish law and order on this raw station on the plains, and it was many years before our city officers felt the need to record the deaths of its citizens.

Cheyenne's history tells us our first years were not made for easy living. Both the weather climate and living climate were not conducive to good health. However, a letter found in the Wyoming State Archives tells us an effort was made by at least one individual to put his sister's mind at rest concerning his life in this new, struggling city. Mr. Jordon wrote, dated November 24, 1867, "I will stay here this winter I think, it is the most healthy climate in the country here. No one knows to die here. Some are talking of sending east for dead men to start a graveyard, we have none here, we have everything else." Of course, with crowded living quarters, no sanitation facilities for water or waste and lawlessness, Cheyenne did have deaths, and a place of burial had to be found.

Our first city cemetery, now termed the Old City Cemetery was located on the north side of Twenty-Eighth Street between Ames and Snyder Avenues. Looking at the history of cemetery sites across the Union Pacific route in Wyoming, one finds a common problem: the first cemetery in each town or city was located quite close to the center of town. This brought the problem of communicable diseases. Each town then grew around the cemeteries, which made the property too valuable for them. In Cheyenne, Major Talbot wanted the land for a racetrack. A racetrack would also give

Cheyenne some tax monies to go into the city budget, so the city council gave the go-ahead to a committee to search for a new cemetery site. There is evidence a sexton was appointed from an account in the *Cheyenne Daily Leader* on January 7, 1871, "When Mr. O'Casey, Sexton, informed us during the past year a total of forty-two burials had been made, and not a single death was from violence!" Cheyenne was started on the path to peaceful growth.

The *Cheyenne Daily Leader* advertised in both June and July 1871 for interested people to meet at the I.C. Whipple Store to discuss where the new cemetery would be located. A plan to place the cemetery east of the Congregational church was evidently objected to, and no further word on this location can be found. At the April 26, 1872 meeting of the board of trustees, a motion by Mr. Fisk asked the committee as a whole to select a place for a burial ground and to locate same, with instructions to report at subsequent meetings. Mr. Sloan reported on May 10, 1872, a site had been selected "about a mile northeast of the city." This site was between Seymour and Russell Avenues and Twenty-Third and Twenty-Fifth Streets. What is now Lakeview Cemetery, a name adopted by newspaper articles and references to the lake to the east and south of the cemetery, was chosen.

Most of the identifiable bodies were moved from the old site to the new cemetery. However, construction crews, while working at the old site, have found bodies that were not moved to the new location. Again, this has been the case in cities across the Union Pacific route in Wyoming. If there was no headstone, family nearby or records, there was no way to determine reburials.

Burials were conducted in the new cemetery but without any supervision reports or records being kept. On June 26, 1874, Dr. George Russell wrote to the cemetery committee, "The present condition of the cemetery and the necessity that existed for having same surveyed and divided into lots, fenced, and to recommend a suitable officer to be found to have charge of the site and register the interments therein." The city surveyor then requested a suitable plat of the grounds that would prove acceptable to the board. In August 1874, Mr. Blackstone, the surveyor, submitted his plat for the cemetery. I have visited many cemeteries throughout the United States and have never found a cemetery platted in the complicated circles, burials on the bias and pathways like Lakeview Cemetery. Perhaps Mr. Blackstone had been to Europe to see plats of the many beautiful English gardens or the mazes that were fashionable, but it is not always easy to find a grave in the configuration of Cheyenne's Lakeview Cemetery.

From October 1874 to April 1875, a series of meetings were held regarding the cemetery. It was decided that the city engineer should sell the lots in the cemetery and use the monies to build a fence around the cemetery and improve the grounds. The fence was to be three boards deep with a cap board on posts eight feet apart. Mr. Hamma and Mr. Whipple took over the task of forming a system of regulations, and Mr. Frank Hunter was appointed sexton of the cemetery. The long-awaited ordinance, dated April 23, 1875, appeared in the newspaper for public notice.

In October 1875, the subject of a burial book was brought up. Mr. Bresnahan asked for the book to show the lots, date of burial, name of deceased, cause of death and any other particulars. The burial book was to be kept in the sexton's office. The first recorded burial in Cheyenne's cemeteries was that of two-year-old Daniel Cassells, the son of George Cassells, on May 22, 1875. Mr. Cassells was on the board of trustees during the time the board was working on the cemetery site and regulations. That means that from at least November 1867 to May 1875, no records of burials in Cheyenne existed, other than the newspaper or church recordings. During the first year of recorded burials, a total of fifty-five persons were buried. By referencing the books today, evidence shows diseases that no longer exist were taking the lives of many children. In July and August 1890 and 1891, cholera took the lives of sixteen children. Smallpox, Diphtheria, croup, peritonitis (gangrene) and cholera have all but disappeared from our health rolls but are found all too often in this burial book. Suicides were quite common, and social diseases were noted as matter of fact.

The lovely iron fencing around Lakeview Cemetery has often been a topic of discussion. When did the iron fence replace the wooden fencing? The answer has been found in the Wyoming State Archives files and a fun-filled interview I conducted with a senior citizen. This citizen told me that he and his twin brother had a hand in getting the new fencing. They were quite small, and it was just before World War I, when he and his brother went to his grandmother's home near the cemetery. She was not at home, but the boys found a box of matches and decided to just walk back home, striking the matches as they went. While walking past the cemetery, the dry grass caught on fire, and when they looked back, the fence was on fire. They got into serious trouble, but thankfully, they were not sent to a reform school. This seems to be the correct timeline, as a letter from the commissioner of finance, City of Cheyenne, to Mr. Herman Gates, the secretary of the Capitol Building Commission, states, "Dear, sir, for all the iron fence now on the state capitol grounds, the city of Cheyenne offers the sum of six hundred

thirty ($630) dollars. If the city of Cheyenne is awarded the fence under this bid, fence will be used to enclose the city burial grounds." In the bid letter, the offer was for a wrought-iron fence, then in place around the capitol grounds in Cheyenne, and bids were to be submitted. The description was: "Eighteen hundred (1,800) feet of fence, with ⅝" square pickets, alternating 2 feet and 4 feet high, placed 4" apart, with tie rods at the top, middle and bottom. The fence is braced every five feet." The fence was condemned for sale on April 20, 1917, and Cheyenne's Lakeview Cemetery received the beautiful antique fencing it has today.

Within Lakeview, there are plots dedicated to various organizations. Among these are two for the Grand Army of the Republic (GAR). The GAR purchased these plots for the burial of Civil War soldiers, especially those who did not have family nearby or the means to pay for their plot. Every city, including Cheyenne, also has what was once known as potter's field for the burial of those without means to pay for it.

A frequent question I am asked is: Where are the different cemeteries in the Cheyenne cemetery complex located? Lakeview Cemetery is the only Cheyenne cemetery located south of Pershing Boulevard. North of Pershing Boulevard, on the far east side, is the Olivet (Catholic) cemetery. West from Olivet are the Odd Fellows Fraternal Organization lots. Directly north of these lots is the Jewish cemetery. To the northwest is Beth El Cemetery, the second Cheyenne city cemetery. The first recorded burial in Beth El occurred on November 19, 1925. All known records and the maintenance of these cemeteries have been turned over to the City of Cheyenne Cemetery Complex Office.

Whenever a history about Wyoming is published, it is a win for those who seek answers to questions about our past. It is my hope this book will provide answers to Lakeview Cemetery's past and a path into the future.

Sharon Lass Field

*Sharon Lass Field is an author, a member and past president of the Cheyenne Genealogical and Historical Society and a volunteer at the Laramie County Library Collections Department. She has served as the script writer and hostess for the Historical Walking Tour of Lakeview Cemetery for many years. Sharon has received awards from the National Federation of Genealogical Societies, including the Ruth Bishop Genealogical Volunteer Hall of Honor Award in 2007, and the United States Daughters of 1812 National History Award in 2018.*

# ACKNOWLEDGEMENTS

T he authors are grateful for the many people who made the compilation of this book a reality. Without the writing, research and assistance of many historians, we could not have written this narrative.

Special thanks go to the staff and volunteers at the Wyoming State Archives, especially Suzi Taylor and Robin Everett.

The efforts of many people who provided information from personal collections are appreciated. We thank Sharon Lass Field for her extensive research on Cheyenne history, a tour of the Lakeview Cemetery and the foreword of this book.

We give special thanks to several people who provided information about their families or other people who are important to them. These individuals include Steve Vandehei and Deidre Newman for information about the Humane Alliance Fountain and their grandfather Earl Vandehei; Deidre Newman for information about her mother, Joy Vandehei; Dan Lyon for his information about the girl guards and about the Japanese section of Lakeview Cemetery; Hisano Bell for her interpretation of the Japanese tombstones; Paula Qualls for information about her great-grandmother Therese Jenkins; and Kim Mill for information about her great-grandfather Joseph Stimson.

We are grateful to the members of the Cheyenne Genealogical and Historical Society for their research and for their presentation of the Lakeview Cemetery Living History Walk.

A very special thank-you goes to Nathan Chapman, the director of the Cemetery Division of the City of Cheyenne. Nathan and his staff provided valuable information about the cemetery and the location of several monuments. The cemetery staff continues to provide loving care for Lakeview Cemetery.

Special thanks to our editor Artie Crisp and others at The History Press for their support and guidance.

Most importantly, we are grateful for our families and spouses. Michael thanks his wife, Amy, who has been the wind beneath his wings, blessing him with her encouragement and fortitude. Starley thanks her husband, Beauford Thompson, for his support in so many ways.

Starley thanks her coauthor, Michael Kassel, for his important research and for his speaking ability, which first inspired her to delve further into the fascinating history of Cheyenne. Michael wishes to thank Starley Talbott, his coauthor, for inspiring him to put into print that which inspired him about the people of Cheyenne and for opening doors he didn't think were possible for him to open on his own.

Lastly, we thank our readers and the many people who continue to inspire us with their love of history.

# INTRODUCTION

Since the late 1800s, Lakeview Cemetery has served as the final resting place for some of the city's early residents and as a repository of the city's and state's history. This history is recorded through the lives of countless people who were pioneers, homesteaders, railroaders, politicians and builders in the capital city of Wyoming. It is here that we can still make a connection to the people who shaped our community so many years ago.

A variety of stones and markers can be found throughout the cemetery. Some memorials are simple markers, while other are more elaborate. Symbols representing the deceased's fraternal affiliations, lifetime interests, important contributions or survivors' sorrow are often etched on the stones. Family lots are sometimes set off by concrete or stone markers or landscaping techniques.

Cheyenne's Lakeview Cemetery is old but still in use. Some of the oldest graves are marked with flat stones with rounded tops. Newer markers are often mixed among the older memorials. There is a small building near the entrance to the cemetery that was formerly used as a holding vault for caskets that were waiting to be interred. This was important during the winter, when blizzards or frozen ground prevented a timely burial. The building is no longer used for this purpose.

Lakeview Cemetery contains the graves of veterans from every war in which the United States has engaged since the middle of the nineteenth century.

Some of these graves are marked with traditional military stones, while others bear reference to the deceased's military service in another form.

It is interesting to note that throughout the United States, there are several cemeteries with the name "Lakeview." Most of them actually do have a lake view. The lake that could once be viewed from the northern and southern sides of Cheyenne's Lakeview Cemetery was partially drained and diverted to Lake Minnehaha in Holiday Park. Houses and businesses eventually filled in that area.

The cemetery is bordered by an intricate iron fence, which replaced the older wooden fence in 1917. There are many trees throughout the cemetery, and some memorials include benches. The grounds are not meant to be visited only in a time of sorrow. Visitors may walk the many paths throughout Lakeview to view its art, history, flora and fauna, as it provides a place of quiet contemplation and solitude.

Many of Cheyenne's historic figures are buried in the several sections of the city's cemetery complex, as well as other cemeteries in the vicinity, including Mountain View Memorial Park, Cheyenne Memorial Gardens, F.E. Warren Air Force Base Cemetery and the National Cemetery.

The authors of this book tell the stories of some of the actors in the historical pageant of our history who are memorialized in Cheyenne's oldest city cemetery, Lakeview Cemetery. Please join them as they describe the lives of the men, women and children who once lived in the community and left a legacy here.

1

# FRANCIS E. WARREN

## *Wyoming Statesman*

On November 25, 1929, the people of Wyoming were shocked at the news that Francis E. Warren had died at his home in Washington, D.C. For the first time since the beginning of its existence, Wyoming was now without the strong and stable guidance of a man who invested everything into the young territory's prosperity, growth and eventual statehood. For more than sixty years, Warren had stood as a paragon of stability, good business acumen and powerful political leadership. Now, the young state had to come to terms that one of its greatest founders was gone, and nothing would be the same.

Francis Emory Warren was born in the tiny rural village of Hinsdale in western Massachusetts on June 20, 1844, to Joseph and Cynthia Warren. The family farm was prosperous in his early childhood, and Warren worked alongside his father and younger brother for years. At the age of fifteen, Warren complained to his father that he wasn't getting enough education to suit his ambitions, so he left the farm and hired himself out to farmers in the area.

When Warren was sixteen years old, he was hired by a local dairy farmer to work alongside several other men. He had grown to be a large man at 160 pounds and was earning a wage of thirteen dollars a month at the dairy farm, milking twelve to fourteen cows twice a day. In the summer, he was consistently busy with the demands of the dairy. In the winter, when things weren't so busy, he pursued his own education. When the farmer who hired him became seriously ill, Warren, who had proved himself a capable manager, was put in charge of the farm. Warren agreed to be the manager but was determined to stay only until he completed his education and found something else to do.

In his seventeenth year, the Civil War broke out, and Warren was eager to join the fight. In September 1862, Warren enlisted in Pittsfield, Massachusetts, and became a private in C Company of the Forty-Ninth Massachusetts Infantry. He fought in several engagements in the war. In late May 1863, Warren's unit was part of a force engaged in Ulysses Grant's campaign against the Confederacy in Vicksburg. What was supposed to be a brief assault turned into a major siege. On May 27, Warren's unit was charged with destroying a Confederate battery as part of a full-scale assault to dislodge the Confederacy's 6,800 soldiers. The attack was poorly coordinated, and the Confederates repelled the assault. In the attack, Warren received a serious scalp wound and was thought to be dead. Fortunately, an alert doctor noticed that he was still living, and he was saved from the fate of being buried alive in a mass grave.

Warren recovered from his injury and continued to serve the Union until he was twenty-one and the war ended. He returned to Massachusetts and found employment as a farm foreman. He learned a great deal about the livestock industry, along with blacksmithing and carpentry.

Gradually, the allure of the West gripped Warren's attention, and he headed west along the Union Pacific Railroad, which was still under construction, traveling almost to the end of the line by May 1868. The railroad had just reached the site of Laramie, and Cheyenne was a bustling boomtown of tents and other temporary buildings. Few at the time thought that Cheyenne would amount to anything, but Warren waived off gloomy predictions about the town's future and settled down, despite the fact that he slept on a bed made of old boxes with a pistol close at hand to defend himself from the bad characters who populated the town. Francis quickly found employment with Asa Converse, a fellow Massachusetts transplant, and worked for his dry goods store beginning in 1871. The business prospered, and the two men became friends and then partners. By 1877, Warren had become so successful that he bought out Converse and renamed the firm the Warren Mercantile Company.

Five years prior to this development, Warren placed his tireless work ethic and optimism into politics by winning a place in the Wyoming territorial legislature as a Republican in 1872. By 1873, he had become the president of the upper house, known as the council, while serving concurrently on the Cheyenne City Council. During his tenure, the city installed its first public

Francis E. Warren, the first elected governor of the state of Wyoming in 1890, also served two terms as the territorial governor of Wyoming and was a United States senator from Wyoming. *Wyoming State Archives, Department of State Parks and Cultural Resources.*

lighting system. Warren also served as the territorial treasurer in 1876 and 1879 and again in 1882 and 1884.

In his personal life, Warren, in 1871, married Helen M. Smith, also of Massachusetts. They were blessed with two children, Frances and Frederick, who were born in 1880 and 1884, respectively.

While continuing his business and political ventures, Warren established the Warren Livestock Company in 1883 and eventually secured 150,000 acres of land, where he raised large numbers of cattle and sheep. As his fortunes increased, so did his expansive involvement in the community. In 1882, he helped establish the Cheyenne Opera House. He also served as president of the Brush-Swan Electric Company, installing the first electric power in Cheyenne. In 1885, Warren became the mayor of Cheyenne.

Warren's tenure as Cheyenne's mayor was short-lived. In January 1885, Wyoming's territorial governor William Hale died. President Chester A. Arthur, who had named Hale governor, was intent to replace him with a Wyoming man before he surrendered the presidency to President-Elect Grover Cleveland. After several weeks of speculation, President Arthur announced his nomination of Francis E. Warren to serve as the territory's governor on February 26. Cheyenne newspaper editors sang the praises of this decision, acknowledging that Warren had an unsullied and unassailable record as a private citizen, businessman and public officer.

For the first few months, Warren's time as territorial governor was unruffled by controversy or major upset. The largest issue was the spread of pleura-pneumonia among national cattle herds. Warren closed the borders of Wyoming Territory to outside cattle unless the animals could be inspected at the Cheyenne Stockyards first.

However, Warren was soon confronted with riots in Rock Springs between white and Chinese coal miners on September 2, 1885. The riots resulted in the deaths of twenty-eight Chinese miners and sent hundreds of others fleeing for their lives. Governor Warren arrived at the scene the next morning and then moved on to Evanston to prevent the further spread of violence. Warren sent a telegram to President Cleveland asking him to dispatch troops to maintain order. The president promptly dispatched three companies from Utah and Fort D.A. Russell in Cheyenne. In the following days, Warren went to Rock Springs to conduct a personal investigation of the tragedy. For the president's efforts in protecting property and restoring order, the Union Pacific expressed its appreciation to him on behalf of Warren. Many suspect it was because of this private support that Warren was able to retain his governorship for twenty months into Cleveland's administration before he was finally replaced by George W. Baxter.

In the legislative assembly of 1886, Warren began making a significant impact on Wyoming's future. Because of his close association with many members of the legislature and the fact that both houses were dominated by the Republicans, he was able to guide policies more effectively. He had recognized the territory's need for a school to help the disabled and a hospital for mental health. Warren asked the legislature to fund a school for the "deaf and dumb" as well as an "insane asylum." The legislature went much further by funding Warren's requests and also adding appropriations for a territorial capitol building and a university.

Warren's request for a school for the blind, deaf and dumb to be built in Cheyenne as soon as fifteen pupils could be located was granted, but it was never built. The insane asylum was established in Evanston. Warren also secured new safety regulations for the territory's coal mines that banned children below a certain age and women from working in the mines, and it required better ventilation and more than one exit from a mine. The legislature, at Warren's prodding, also established rules for acquiring water for irrigation and divided the territory into water districts to be overseen by commissioners who were selected directly by the governor. Warren also took advantage of new federal laws that allowed for the taxation of lands owned by the railroad, homesteaders or others, resulting in territory gaining a stable source of funding. While not everyone was pleased with the results of the legislature of 1886, Warren could take credit for significant improvements for the territory's benefit. Regardless of Warren's success, President Grover Cleveland was intent on replacing him with a fellow Democrat. He did so in November with George W. Baxter.

Warren's hiatus from politics was short-lived. When Republican Benjamin Harrison became president in 1888, he restored Warren to the governorship of Wyoming Territory. Warren and his allies, including Joseph M. Carey, began the ambitious plan to have Wyoming elevated to statehood. Carey, as the elected representative of Wyoming Territory to Congress, asked that body to consider the prospect of statehood. There were questions about whether Wyoming had achieved the minimum of sixty thousand citizens to qualify, so the Congress declined to act.

Governor Warren called for a territory-wide election for delegates for a constitutional convention in July 1889. In September, forty-nine delegates met at the capitol to draft the founding document for statehood. The people of Wyoming ratified the new constitution in a special election called by Warren on November 5. In March 1890, Joseph M. Carey took the finished constitution to the floor of the U.S. House of Representatives and advocated for statehood. Debates regarding the true population of Wyoming and the constitution's provision allowing women the right to vote echoed in the chamber. Eventually, the House voted to accept Wyoming's statehood, as did the Senate. On July 10, 1890, President Benjamin Harrison signed the bill, and Wyoming became the forty-fourth state to join the Union.

Francis E. Warren's popularity ensured that he would be elected the first governor of the State of Wyoming. He served as governor for two months before he was selected to serve a two-year term as Wyoming's second senator, joining Joseph M. Carey in Washington. Warren and Carey soon found their relationship while working together to be difficult. Their conflict was heightened because of the Free Silver issue wracking Congress at the time. Wyoming's citizens were in support of adding silver to the U.S. Treasury to back the national currency, whereas the national Republican Party was adamant in maintaining the gold standard. Carey chose to back the national party, while Warren publicly deferred to his constituency on the matter, thus placing the two men on opposite sides.

Another grave issue that caused conflict between Carey and Warren was the fallout of the Johnson County War in 1892. The invasion, instigated by many members of the Wyoming Stock Growers Association, was a conflict between Wyoming's cattle barons and smaller ranchers in Northern Wyoming. Both Carey and Warren were members of the powerful Wyoming Stock Growers Association. When Carey and Warren were confronted about their potential role in the invasion, Carey kept quiet and went as far as destroying his papers regarding the matter, while Warren publicly stated his support for the stock growers, if not for their actions.

Warren quietly left office as a Wyoming senator for a time, because the bitterly divided Wyoming legislature could not agree on his replacement. However, Warren's political influence saw him returned to the United States

Senate in 1895, and he remained there until his death. At the same time, the Wyoming legislature ejected Carey, who blamed Warren's powerful political machinery within the state for his ousting. The two men remained powerful political adversaries until Warren cast his support behind Carey's son Robert as Wyoming's prospective governor in 1918.

Fully in control of Wyoming politics at home, Warren used his unchallenged position in Washington to advance his goals for the state. He held several very powerful positions in the Senate, each of which he used to Wyoming's benefit. As chairman of the Senate Military Affairs Committee, he strengthened and enlarged Fort D.A. Russell in Cheyenne and kept Fort Mackenzie and Fort Washakie in full operation long after these frontier posts were necessary. As chairman of the Committee on Irrigation and Reclamation of Public Lands, he fought hard to get federal lands turned over to the states, though this effort was not successful. He created a small scandal when he hired Leona Wells as the first woman Senate staff member. She served as his secretary for the next thirty years, by which time she was joined by two hundred other women Senate staff members.

The early years of the twentieth century were both joyful and heart-rending for Senator Warren. In April 1902, his wife, Helen, died after a long illness. In January 1905, his eldest daughter, Frances, married the dashing Captain John J. Pershing in Washington, D.C. Though no history officially gives credit to Warren for his influence, President Teddy Roosevelt advanced Pershing from the rank of captain to the rank of brigadier general ahead of nine hundred senior officers who were qualified for the position.

Senator Francis Warren, age sixty-seven, married thirty-five-year-old Clara Morgan of Groton, Connecticut, on July 12, 1911. They were entertained by President Taft at the White House after their nuptials.

In 1915, Warren was devastated by the death of his daughter, Frances, and three of his grandchildren when the Pershing home at the Presidio in San Francisco caught fire. All four were buried at the family plot in Cheyenne's Lakeview Cemetery. General Pershing and Senator Warren remained close after the tragedy. When Warren became the ranking minority member of the Appropriations Committee, a position he held from 1911 to 1929, he was in the perfect position to help fund and equip the American Expeditionary Force that General Pershing would lead after America's entry into World War I.

Through the 1920s, Warren continued to take care of Wyoming on the national scene and at home. He strongly supported the Nineteenth Amendment, which gave women the right to vote, and was just as equally

The funeral of Francis E. Warren at Lakeview Cemetery. *Wyoming State Archives, Department of State Parks and Cultural Resources.*

opposed the Twentieth Amendment, which established the prohibition of alcohol in the United States. He consistently voted for strong tariffs to protect the agriculture and livestock industries and supported the policies of presidents Warren G. Harding and Calvin Coolidge.

On November 13, 1929, Warren was reportedly confined to his home in Washington with a cold. His situation deteriorated rapidly, and his illness developed into a combination of bronchitis and pneumonia. On November 24, 1929, at the age of eighty-five, Warren died, with his wife, Clara, son Frederick and General Pershing at his bedside. Warren was given a funeral service in the Senate chamber in the National Capitol. He had served longer than any U.S. senator up to that time and was the last veteran of the American Civil War to do so. Congress had also conferred the Congressional Medal of Honor to him on September 30, 1893, for the valor he displayed thirty years earlier at the Siege of Port Hudson.

The impact that Francis E. Warren had on the city of Cheyenne and the State of Wyoming is incomparable. Our city and state continue to bear his influence in the many buildings he was involved with in Cheyenne, including the capitol building, the Plains Hotel, the Majestic building, the Nagel-Warren mansion and many other edifices in the downtown area.

One of Cheyenne's prime avenues bears his name, and the avenue north of his final resting place in Lakeview Cemetery bears the name of his son-in-law, Pershing. Even more enduring is his role in the nascent history of

*Above*: The Nagle-Warren Mansion on Seventeenth Street was purchased by Francis E. Warren after it had been constructed by Erasmus Nagel from stone that had been rejected for use in the building of the state capitol. *J.E. Stimson Collection, Wyoming State Archives, Department of State Parks and Cultural Resources.*

*Right*: The Nagle-Warren Mansion on Seventeenth Street as it looked in 2022. A bronze statue, *Mountain Love*, of a mountain lion and her cubs, by sculptor Christine Knapp, was recently installed there as part of a citywide bronze sculpture project. The donors of the bronze statue are Art and Carol Merrill. *Starley Talbott photograph.*

our territory and the impact he had on the national level while serving as Wyoming's senator. His service was of such a nature that the president of the United States Herbert Hoover decided to honor him by renaming Fort D.A. Russell in his honor on January 1, 1930. The base was designated Francis E. Warren Air Force Base in 1949.

Francis E. Warren was buried in the Warren family at plot at Lakeview Cemetery. A large granite monument marks the final resting place of one of Wyoming's "Grand Old Men."

# 2

# THERESE ALBERTA JENKINS

## *Suffrage Advocate and Statehood Orator*

The voice of Therese Jenkins was loud and clear when she spoke at the Wyoming statehood celebration on July 23, 1890. She had practiced her speech as her husband drove their wagon farther away from her, telling her to speak louder.

Therese was born on May 1, 1853, in Wisconsin, the daughter of Peter and Cleantha Parkinson. She became a teacher before she moved to Wyoming to marry James F. Jenkins, a Cheyenne merchant, on December 20, 1877. The couple had three children, May, Elsie, Horace and Agnes Wyoming.

After moving to Cheyenne, she became interested in working to secure voting rights for women. She was a charter member of the Woman's Christian Temperance Union and was active in the First Presbyterian Church in Cheyenne.

Women in Wyoming had been granted the right to vote by the territorial legislature in 1869. The Wyoming Constitutional Convention met in Cheyenne in 1889 and reaffirmed the right of women to vote and included that right in the state constitution. However, there were some delegates opposed to the inclusion of the clause granting women the right to vote. Therese's husband, James, had been informed of the opposition at his store in Cheyenne. He went home for lunch and told Therese about the problem. He hitched up his horse and buggy and drove Therese around town, where she went door to door asking several of the prominent women in town to go to the capitol to protest the resolution to remove women's voting rights. They were able to obtain a promise from the man who had introduced the resolution to withdraw it from consideration.

Therese Jenkins was credited with saving the women's suffrage movement in Wyoming and delivering a statehood speech on July 23, 1890. *Wyoming State Archives, Department of State Parks and Cultural Resources.*

Unfortunately, Therese was unable to join the force of women at the capitol because she went into labor during the buggy ride around town. A few hours later, she gave birth to a baby girl and named the child Agnes Wyoming Jenkins.

On July 10, 1890, a bill making Wyoming the forty-fourth state to join the union was signed by President Benjamin Harrison. Because of Therese Jenkins's effort to save women's suffrage for the new state, officials invited her to deliver the keynote address at the statehood celebration. She wrote and memorized her speech and then practiced it while James and baby Agnes moved the buggy farther away, signaling when Therese could be heard and understood.

The official celebration of statehood on July 23, 1890, was attended by nearly five thousand people and included a two-mile parade featuring troops and bands, along with many carriages and floats. On one large float rode forty-two young women representing the nation's older states. The parade led to the capitol, in front of which a large throng had gathered for the principal program of the day.

Jenkins delivered her much anticipated speech, a review of the struggle for women's suffrage. The *Cheyenne Leader* stated the next day that her address was the most forceful and eloquent of the day, although it conceded that at one point, she was carried away by a "fairest and rarest flight of oratory."

Some excerpts from Jenkins speech include:

> *On behalf of the ladies present and in the name of many who are not with us today, I am requested to make this expression of our appreciation of the great benefit conferred upon us at your hands and confirmed by the Congress of these United States. Happy are our hearts today, and our lips but sound a faint echo of the gratitude within our bosoms. While we rejoice with you that our young commonwealth has been permitted to place upon this beautiful banner her bright prophetic star, how much more reason have we for enthusiastic demonstration.*
>
> *The republican spirit of 1890, with a generosity unrivaled in all the annals of political economy, has admitted into the national jurisprudence,*

*the voice of woman. We have been placed upon the very summit of freedom and the broad plain of universal equality. Think ye that our tongues are silent or that we have no need to sing our anthems of praise? History chronicles no such an event on all its pages, and the bells of the past ring out no such victory.*

*We have never been compelled to petition or protest; we have ever been treated with a patient hearing and our practical suggestions have been most courteously received and in the future we but desire a continuance of these favors. We ask of our law makers just laws for the enlargement and perpetuity of our educational facilities; we ask of our legislators wise and magnanimous measures for the erection and maintainance [sic] of our benevolent institution; we ask of you laws for the better protection of the moral as well as physical natures of our boys and girls, even though the maverick be neglected, and, taxpayers and burden bearers that we are, may we not expect the proper enforcement of these laws as well as the framing of them. We have, it is true, many lessons to learn and possibly many mistakes to make, but shall we not choose for our instructors those have had our best interests at heart, who seeing the need may plan for the result. We, no doubt, will be advised by many factions, some declaring we are behind in our social and moral reforms, others that we outspeed [sic] public sentiment, but the experiment is ours, and with us it will succeed or fail....*

*Bartholdi's statue of liberty enlightening the world is fashioned in the form of a woman and placed upon a pedestal carved from the everlasting granite of the New England hills, but the women of Wyoming have been placed upon a firmer foundation and hold a more brilliant torch....*

*These words of thankfulness would be incomplete were we to neglect to utter the sentiments of our hearts in enumerating among our noble friends the names of the framers of our constitution...and in this galaxy of stars which every woman wears today a diadem of gems shines out, the fairest and rarest of them all, F.E. Warren and J.M. Carey, and ye who applaud say never again a prophet has honor save in his own country....*

*And may that beautiful bow of color which spanned our eastern boundary at the golden sunset hour of July 10, 1890, be but a faint promise of the prosperity, the stability, the harmony of our magnificent domain, guided (not governed) by the hand of man clasped in the hand of woman.*

Jenkins did not rest on her laurels following her speech in 1890. In 1892, she was elected to attend the Republican National Convention in Minneapolis. In 1893, she spoke in Denver and other Colorado towns, campaigning for a referendum on women's suffrage in support of Colorado becoming the second state in the nation to grant women the right to vote.

When Jenkins attended the convention of the National American Woman's Suffrage Association in 1919, she was implored to ask Wyoming governor Robert Carey to call a special session of the legislature to ratify the Nineteenth Amendment to the Constitution. He agreed to do so, and Wyoming became the twenty-seventh state to vote for the amendment's ratification.

Following her death on February 28, 1936, Therese A. Jenkins was honored by the Wyoming Centennial Lasting Legacy Project with a plaque on her gravestone at Lakeview Cemetery citing her accomplishments:

> *Credited with Saving Woman's Suffrage in the State of Wyoming; Chosen to Make Statehood Speech on 23 July 1890; First Woman Delegate in Nation to Republican National Convention in Minneapolis in 1892.*

# 3

# ESTHER HOBART MORRIS

## *A Streetcar Named Esther*

**E**sther Hobart Morris lived more than half of her life in the eastern United States before moving west, where she made a name for herself in the gold mining town of South Pass City, Wyoming Territory.

Esther Hobart McQuigg was born on August 8, 1812, in Tioga County, New York. Esther lived her early childhood on the family farm, where her mother died when Esther was fourteen. After her father's death in 1833, Esther lived with her sister in Owego, New York.

In Owego, Esther opened a millinery shop. After a few years operating her successful business, providing hats for other women, Esther married Artemas Slack on December 15, 1841. Following her marriage, Esther closed the millinery shop, just a few months before she became the mother of Archibald Artemas Slack on October 2, 1842. Tragedy struck the young family when Esther's husband, Artemas, died in the spring of 1843.

As a young widow, Esther remained in New York for a time, but she subsequently decided to move to Peru, Illinois, with her son, Archie, where she opened a millinery shop. In 1846, she married John Morris. In 1849, a son named John was born to the couple. Two years later, Esther gave birth to twins, Robert Charles and Edward John, on November 8, 1851. Tragedy struck again when her son John died of cholera in 1852.

Esther cared for her family and worked part time sewing and making hats, while her husband was often traveling for business. In 1860, Esther's son Archie attended school in Chicago. He worked as a printer and went by the name E.A. Slack.

The Civil War brought more changes for the family, and E.A. "Archie" Slack enlisted to fight on the Union side of the conflict in 1861. Archie survived the war and ended his service on July 9, 1864, and returned to school in Chicago. He began his future newspaper career there as a journalist with the *Chicago Sun*.

By 1868, Archie had graduated from college, worked for a newspaper and returned to Peru, Illinois. Along with his stepfather, John Morris, Archie became interested in traveling to Wyoming after the *Chicago Tribune* touted riches were available in the gold rush in Wyoming Territory. In April 1868, John and Archie traveled to Wyoming Territory, while Esther moved to New York, where she would remain until the men could become established in the West.

In South Pass City, John Morris and E.A. Slack purchased mining and business property. E.A was appointed constable of South Pass City on December 18, 1868, and became an agent for a lumber company. In the spring of 1869, Esther Morris and her son Ed arrived in Wyoming Territory.

Esther Morris was fifty-six years old when she set foot in South Pass City in May. She was nearly six feet tall and was described as being self-assured and dignified. Soon after her arrival, Esther moved with her family into a twenty-four-by-twenty-six-foot log cabin. Her son Robert joined the family in South Pass City in July.

At approximately the same time, territorial leaders were convening in Cheyenne. John Campbell had been appointed governor of Wyoming Territory. Campbell named Cheyenne the temporary capital of the territory and the home of the first judicial district court in May 1869. Subsequently, the second court was created in Laramie. The third district court was established in South Pass City, and E.A. "Archie" Slack was appointed the clerk of court.

Wyoming's first territorial legislative session commenced on October 12, 1869, in Cheyenne. William Bright of South Pass City was elected the council president and introduced a women's suffrage bill. Historical accounts claim that Bright believed in women's suffrage for a variety of reasons. Since the nation would not repeal Black suffrage, which he adamantly opposed, he reasoned that white women should also be able to vote.

The bill was debated and amended several times, but passed in the legislature and was signed into law on December 10, 1869, reading as follows:

*Be it enacted by the Council and House of Representatives of the Territory of Wyoming: Section 1. That every woman of the age of twenty-one years, residing in this territory, may at every election to be holden under the laws thereof, cast her vote. And her rights to the elective franchise and to hold office shall be the same under the election laws of the territory, as those of electors. Sec. 2. This act shall take effect and be in force from and after its passage.*

Even though Esther Morris is sometimes credited with being a major factor in the success of women's suffrage, because she supposedly exacted a promise from William Bright to introduce a suffrage bill in Wyoming, she is believed to have played a minor role in the bill's passage.

According to myth, Morris held a tea party in her home in South Pass City in September 1869 for forty members of the community. During the tea party, Morris is said to have received a promise from Bright to introduce the suffrage bill. Most contemporary historians give Bright major credit for the bill and believe there was never a tea party at Esther's home in South Pass City.

A letter dated December 27, 1869, written by Robert Morris and published in the *Revolution*, a women's suffrage publication, explains what probably happened:

*Mr. Bright returned to his home in this place a few days ago, and Mrs. Morris and myself, as the only open advocates here of Woman's Suffrage, resolved ourselves into a committee and called on him to render our congratulations and thanks for his services in our behalf as well as for all true lovers of Equal Rights.*

*We found Mr. Bright in a comfortable log cabin with his good wife and little son. We met with a cordial reception, and he expressed himself pleased that there were some persons here who endorsed his views on Woman Suffrage.*

*Mr. Bright told us, "I have never thought much about it, nor have I been converted by a woman's lecture or newspaper, for I have never heard a woman speak from the podium and never read* The Revolution. *I knew that it was a new issue, and a live one, and with a strong feeling that it was just, I determined to use all my influence in my power to have the bill passed." (The* Revolution, *January 18, 1870)*

As for Esther Hobart Morris, she became a national figure in the woman's suffrage movement due to her appointment as a justice of the peace at South Pass City, Wyoming, beginning in February 1870. She served for eight and a half months and heard twenty-seven cases. Most of her cases were disagreements over debts, although ten cases involved assaults.

Morris declined to seek election for justice of the peace, though she stated that holding the job had demonstrated that women could perform well in elected offices. In a letter to those attending a suffrage convention in January 1871 in Washington, D.C., Morris wrote the following:

> *So far as woman suffrage has progressed in this Territory, we are entirely indebted to men. To William H. Bright belongs the honor of presenting the woman suffrage bill; and it was our district Judge, Hon. John W. Kingham, who proposed my appointment as a justice of the peace and the trial of women as jurors.*
>
> *Circumstances have transpired to make my position as a Justice of the Peace a test of woman's ability to hold public office, and I feel that my work has been satisfactory, although I have often regretted I was not better qualified to fill the position. Like all pioneers, I have labored more in faith and hope.*
>
> *I have assisted in drawing a grand and petit jury, deposited a ballot, and helped canvass the votes after election, and in performing all these duties I do not know as I have neglected my family any more than in ordinary shopping, and I must admit that I have been better paid for the services rendered than for any I have ever performed. In some thirty civil actions tried before me, there has been not one appeal taken, and the judgement was affirmed in the court above, and in the criminal cases also before me, there has been no call for a jury.*
>
> *My idea of the woman question in Wyoming is that while we enjoy the privilege of the elective franchise, we have not been sufficiently educated up to it. The election here and agitation of woman's voting has caused us to think and has placed us far in advance of what we were, and I now think that we shall be able to sustain the position which has been granted to us.*

Wyoming went on to become the forty-fourth state admitted to the Union, and it retained women's suffrage within its constitution. Esther Morris presented a forty-four-star silk flag to Governor Francis E. Warren during the statehood celebration on July 23, 1890.

In 1960, upon the request of Senator Lester Hunt, a statue of Esther Morris was placed in the rotunda of the United States Capitol. On December 8, 1963, a bronze replica of the statue was placed in front of the Wyoming State Capitol. Senator Hunt had recommended Morris for the honor because she had been the first woman justice of peace in the United States, along with the myth of "Esther's Tea Party" and her influence in Wyoming's passage of women's suffrage. During the 2019 restoration of the Wyoming State Capitol, the Esther Morris statue, along with a statue of Chief Washakie, was moved inside.

In the meantime, back in South Pass City, Esther Morris cast her first vote in an election on September 6, 1870. Esther's term as justice of the peace ended on October 31, 1870. E.A. Slack had married Sarah Neely on September 22, 1870, and they made their home in South Pass City before they moved to Laramie, Wyoming Territory, in 1871, where E.A. became the proprietor of the *Laramie Daily Independent*.

Esther had received an invitation to attend the January 1871 National Woman Suffrage Convention in Washington, D.C., but she declined to attend the meeting. She later attended the American Suffrage Association Convention in San Francisco in 1872.

After difficulties with her life in South Pass City, Esther joined E.A. in Laramie. Her son Robert has also relocated to Laramie. John Morris and his son Ed remained in South Pass City. A few years later, Esther attended the National Woman Suffrage Convention in Philadelphia in 1876.

John Morris died on September 29, 1877, and was buried in South Pass City. In 1902, John's remains were moved to Lakeview Cemetery in Cheyenne.

E.A. Slack had moved to Cheyenne in 1876 to become the publisher of the *Cheyenne Sun*. Esther had moved several times, including to New York and Illinois. In 1881, Esther moved to Cheyenne, where she spent several months at the home of E.A. and Sarah Slack. By 1883, she was living in the home on Warren Avenue in Cheyenne, which she would occupy until her death.

Esther Hobart Morris is honored for her role in securing votes for women with this sign near her former residence in Cheyenne on Warren Avenue. *Starley Talbott photograph.*

This Cheyenne streetcar bearing the name *Esther*, in honor of Esther Hobart Morris, is available for a historic tour through Cheyenne. *Starley Talbott photograph.*

Esther remained active in Cheyenne, maintaining a garden, reading and enjoying her two granddaughters, Harriet and Dora, children of E.A. and Sara Slack. In 1895, she was selected as a delegate and attended the National Convention of the Republican Leagues in Cleveland, Ohio.

On the night of April 2, 1902, Esther died, only a few months short of her ninetieth birthday. Her remains were interred at Lakeview Cemetery, along with those of many of her illustrious family members.

In a tribute to Esther Morris, one of the streetcar trolleys used to take locals and visitors around Cheyenne to learn about historic sites is named *Esther*. Riders pass by the house where she lived on Warren Avenue. Next to Esther's house is a plaque honoring her service as a judge and an advocate for women's rights.

# 4

# ARCHIBALD ARTEMAS "E.A." SLACK

## *Co-Founder of a Frontier Celebration*

I n 1897, Cheyenne's leaders were interested in expanding the growth
and potential of Cheyenne as more than just a town along the tracks
of the Union Pacific Railroad. However, the railroad continued to
play an important role in the city's progress.

A Union Pacific employee and a newspaper editor teamed up to present
a unique idea for sponsoring an event that would contribute to Cheyenne's
economy and bring visitors to town. The future event would come to be
known as Cheyenne Frontier Days™.

By that time, the editor was known as Colonel E.A. Slack. He had come
a long way from his birth as Archibald Artemas Slack in Owego, New York,
on October 2, 1842, to Esther and Artemas Slack. He would be known over
the years by several names, but his professional title came to be E.A. Slack.
But he was always called Archie by his mother, Esther.

Archie Slack's father died before he turned one year old. His mother
moved to Illinois, where she married John Morris in 1846 and became
known, thereafter, as Esther Hobart Morris. The couple became the parents
of John in 1849 and twin sons, Robert and Edward, in 1851. John Morris
died of cholera in 1852.

The family lived in Peru, Illinois, as the boys were growing up. At the
age of eighteen, Archie attended Chicago University. He also worked as a
printer and was known by the name of Edward Archibald, or E.A. Slack.
His studies and work were interrupted when he enlisted in the Union Army
in June 1861, after the Civil War broke out. E.A. served in Company H,

Nineteenth Illinois Volunteer Regiment. His service in the military ended in 1864, and he returned to school in Chicago.

Along with his university classes, E.A. began his long and illustrious newspaper career as a journalist with the *Chicago Sun*. After graduating in 1866, he spent the summer in Peru, Illinois, and then attended Soldier's College in Fulton for a short time. Then he began work as a printer in Carlinville, Illinois, in 1867.

After a few months, E.A.'s work as a printer was interrupted when he returned to Peru to join his stepfather, John Morris, who had become interested in the gold rush in South Pass City, Wyoming Territory. The two men decided to venture west and join the quest for gold, arriving in South Pass City in the spring of 1868.

John and E.A. soon found that gold was not as easy to find in South Pass City as it had been touted. They eventually purchased mining and business property, while E.A. found work in construction and became an agent for a lumber company.

People throughout Wyoming Territory were involved in various activities. Territorial leaders convened in Cheyenne in May 1869. Cheyenne was named the temporary capital, and three judicial district courts were established in Wyoming Territory. E.A. Slack was appointed clerk of the third judicial district court in South Pass City. After his mother and stepbrothers arrived that spring, E.A. hired Robert Morris to clerk for him at the district court, and he hired Ed Morris to work as a bookkeeper at the lumber company.

In February 1870, the Morris family became noteworthy in the history of the nation. E.A. Slack, district court clerk, swore in his mother, Esther Hobart Morris, as justice of the peace in South Pass City, Wyoming Territory. Esther became the first woman in the nation to hold a judicial office, where she served until October 31, 1870.

Meanwhile, E.A. had traveled back to Illinois, where he married Sarah Neely on September 22, 1870, at the governor's mansion in Springfield. The couple spent their honeymoon in St. Louis and returned to live in South Pass City. E.A. resigned as district court clerk and continued with his lumber business.

On May 24, 1871, E.A. Slack became the editor of the *South Pass News*. In June, he purchased the newspaper and became the publisher. Unfortunately, a fire at the print shop in the fall ended E.A.'s tenure as a publisher in South Pass City, as the newspaper was forced to close down. In December, E.A. moved to Laramie and became the proprietor of the *Laramie Daily Independent*. Sarah and the couple's infant son, Charles, joined

E.A. in Laramie a few months later, though Charles died on August 23, 1872. The same year, Robert Morris and his mother, Esther, joined the family in Laramie. In 1873, E.A. and Sarah had a second child, Esther, who died a few weeks after her birth.

As a newspaper editor, E.A. was active in political issues, and he was a member of the Republican Party. In 1876, he moved to Cheyenne to become editor of the *Cheyenne Daily Sun*, where he embarked on a career as one of the most colorful and powerful editors in Wyoming.

Following E.A.'s move to Cheyenne, Esther left Laramie and lived for a time in New York and Illinois. It was reported that she was happy to receive news of the birth of a daughter, Harriett Louise Slack, to E.A. and Sarah on June 15, 1878. Both Esther

E.A. Slack, the son of Esther Hobart Morris, was a newspaper publisher in Cheyenne. *Wyoming State Archives, Department of State Parks and Cultural Resources.*

Morris and her son Robert eventually moved to Cheyenne in 1882. Robert began working for the territorial government and purchased a house at 2114 Warren Avenue in Cheyenne. Esther lived there for the rest of her life, and she enjoyed gardening and spending time with her granddaughters there. Sarah had given birth to Dora Frances Slack on August 15, 1885.

The issue of statehood for Wyoming became a passionate cause for E.A. Slack. He advocated for immediate statehood in 1889. Following the state territorial legislative convention, territorial representative Joseph M. Carey introduced a Wyoming statehood bill in the United States House of Representatives. The bill passed the House and Senate and was signed on July 10, 1890, by President Benjamin Harrison, making Wyoming the forty-fourth state.

The official celebration of statehood took place on July 23, 1890. The *Cheyenne Daily Sun* reported on the festivities in a special edition of the newspaper. During the celebration, Esther Morris presented a forty-four-star flag to territorial governor Francis E. Warren. In a tribute to his mother in his newspaper, E.A. wrote the following, which later contributed to the confusion and myth of the role his mother had actually played in the women's suffrage movement:

*Mrs. Esther Morris, one of Wyoming's historical characters, who is regarded as the "mother" of the woman suffrage movement in this state, and who is otherwise honored and respected for her great ability and heroic womanhood, was by general consent accorded the post of honor, and made the presentation to Governor Warren on behalf of the women of Wyoming.*

By 1895, E.A. Slack had purchased the *Cheyenne Daily Leader* newspaper and combined his two newspapers into one, which he called the *Cheyenne Daily Sun-Leader*. Eventually, he changed the name of his newspaper to the *Cheyenne Daily Leader*. In 1904, Slack sold the enterprise to his son-in-law, Wallace Bond, and Harry Clark. E.A.'s daughter, Harriet, had married Wallace Bond in 1899.

One of the lasting legacies of the Slack and Morris families was the creation and continued success of Cheyenne Frontier Days™. The *Cheyenne Daily Sun Leader* reported on the organization of the western celebration to promote Cheyenne. The newspaper gave credit for the concept of the celebration to Frederick W. Angier, a Union Pacific agent. Slack supported the formation of the festival and published the Frontier Day edition of the *Cheyenne Daily Sun Leader* on September 23, 1897.

The next years in Cheyenne were busy with the continued building of the city. E.A.'s stepbrother Robert Morris was involved in raising money for the construction of the Carnegie Library and had served as the secretary of the Wyoming State Historical Society in 1897.

E.A. and Sarah's second daughter, Dora, married William R. Dubois, a prominent Cheyenne architect, on November 5, 1904. Thus, the legacy of the family of Esther Hobart Morris passed to the next generation. Esther died on April 2, 1902. E.A. retired from the newspaper business in 1904 and died on March 23, 1907.

W.E. Chaplin, E.A.'s longtime friend and competitor, honored him in the *Cheyenne Daily Leader* with a lengthy tribute, including this brief summary:

*Colonel Slack was one of the strong men of Wyoming....His influence in the making of the history of Cheyenne and Wyoming will never be forgotten.*

# 5

# WILLIAM R. DUBOIS I, II AND III

## *A Trio of Leaders*

Three generations of men with the surname Dubois provided leadership and innovation to the community of Cheyenne. Beginning in 1901, their contributions to the city continued for more than a century.

## WILLIAM ROBERT DUBOIS I

Twenty-two-year-old architect William Dubois arrived in Cheyenne to supervise the construction of the Carnegie Library. In the following years, he served as the architect for numerous Cheyenne buildings.

Dubois was born in Chicago on November 15, 1879. He was trained as an architect and worked in New Mexico for a time. After working in Cheyenne as an architect for two years, William married Dora Frances Slack on November 5, 1904. Dora was the daughter of E.A. and Sarah Slack and the granddaughter of Esther Hobart Morris. Thus, the families of Morris, Slack and Dubois were united.

William Dubois established himself as one of the premier architects of the early twentieth century in Cheyenne. Some of his historic contributions to the city include the following:

William Dubois I was a prominent architect in Cheyenne. *J.E. Stimson Collection, Wyoming State Archives, Department of State Parks and Cultural Resources.*

## Government Buildings

- Wyoming State Capitol: The construction of the original capitol was completed in 1888, with architect David W. Gibbs heading up the project. The first additions of east and west wings, also designed by Gibbs, were completed in 1890. In 1915, additional space was again needed for the capitol. William Dubois was the architect for this final phase, which was completed in March 1917.
- The city and county building was completed in 1919.
- The federal building, at 308 West Twenty-First Street, was constructed in 1932.
- The supreme court building, at 2301 Capitol Avenue, was erected in 1937 as a project with the Federal Emergency Administration of Public Works.
- Several buildings at the Cheyenne Horticultural Field Station were constructed beginning in 1928.

## Schools

- McCormick Junior High School, at 2001 Capitol Avenue, was constructed in 1929. The original building contained thirty-eight classrooms, a gymnasium, a library, a cafeteria and an auditorium. The building was later purchased by the State of Wyoming and renamed the Emerson State office building in honor of Frank Emerson.
- Cheyenne High School, at 2810 House Avenue, was constructed in 1922 and later served as the administration building for Cheyenne Public Schools. Dubois served as the architect for the original building.
- Churchill Elementary School, at 510 West Twenty-Ninth Street, was constructed in 1911.
- Gibson Clark Elementary School, at Twenty-Eighth and House Streets, was built in 1920 and later became part of the administrative complex.
- Johnson Elementary School, at 712 House Avenue, was built in 1923. It later became Johnson Junior High School.

## Business Buildings

- The Plains Hotel, at 1600 Central Avenue, was one of the most elaborately furnished hotels in the western states when it opened on March 9, 1911. The hotel was five stories high and contained one hundred sleeping rooms, each with a telephone. There were also offices and shops on the main floor. Designed by architect William Dubois, the hotel was the pride of the city.
- The Majestic building, at Sixteenth Street at Capitol Avenue, was constructed in 1907 as the First National Bank. When the bank closed in 1924, the building was redesigned as an office and store building.
- The Gleason building, constructed in 1913 at 1601 Central Avenue, has housed many Cheyenne enterprises, including the Grier Furniture Company.
- The Hynds building, at Sixteenth Street and Capitol Avenue, was constructed of concrete and steel in 1922.

- The Boyd building, at 1720 Carey Avenue, was built in 1911 and stood for many years as Cheyenne's tallest office building.
- The Atlas Theatre, at 211 West Lincolnway, was originally constructed in 1887. In 1907, William Dubois served as the architect for the remodeling of the building to provide spaces for several enterprises, including a theater.

## *Homes*

- The Strader home was built in 1908 at 715 East Seventeenth Street in the Spanish style.
- The Hinkle home, at 2722 Carey Avenue, has had several owners over the years.
- The Charles Hirsig home, at 2800 Carey Avenue, has also been owned by several families.
- The Bishop's Residence, at Carey Avenue and Pershing Boulevard, was built in 1939 as the residence for the bishop of the Diocese of Cheyenne. It is a red brick home that was constructed in the Georgian style.

During their marriage, William and Dora had five children. These children included William Robert Dubois II, born in 1905, died in 1982; Berthe Frances, born in 1907, died in 2004; George Allen, born in 1909, died in 1999; Dora Isabel, born in 1917, died in 1983; and Edward Neely, born in 1925, died in 2002.

Dora Slack Dubois was killed in a train/car accident in Cheyenne in 1938, a tragedy that her devoted husband never recovered from, according to reports. William's daughter, Dora Isabel, cared for him until he died on May 13, 1953.

# WILLIAM ROBERT DUBOIS II

The second William Robert Dubois was born in 1905. He grew up in Cheyenne and married Elinor Noh. The couple had four children, William Robert Dubois III, Josephine, Susan and Thomas.

William Robert Dubois II was known as "Robert" and apparently lived his life quietly, as very little was written about him. He served as a chairman and head of the board of directors of the Stock Growers National Bank (now the Wells Fargo Bank).

Elinor Dubois died on March 16, 1979, and William Robert died on April 28, 1982.

# WILLIAM ROBERT DUBOIS III

The son of Robert and Elinor Dubois, the grandson of William and Dora Dubois, the great-grandson of E.A. and Sarah Slack and the great-great-grandson of Esther Hobart Morris, William Robert Dubois III was born on September 8, 1936. He grew up in Cheyenne and achieved multiple accomplishments during his eighty-five years of life.

Known as "Bill" throughout his storied career, he was a teacher, author, community activist, goodwill ambassador, musician and friend of Frontier Days. He received a bachelor's degree from Northwestern University in 1958 and a master's degree from the University of Wyoming in 1963.

Bill Dubois taught social studies and American history in Cheyenne schools for thirty-seven years and was the past president of the Cheyenne Education Association. He authored and coauthored many articles focusing on Cheyenne.

He garnered many honors, including outstanding teacher of the year in 1968, man of the year from the chamber of commerce in 1979, the Phi Delta Kappa award for excellence in teaching and civic work in 1988 and the Governor's Arts Award in 1991.

As an outstanding advocate for Cheyenne Frontier Days, Bill was the founding chairman of the Cheyenne Frontier Days™ Old West Museum board. In his years of service for the annual celebration, he was a member of the general committee and served on the Indian Committee for thirty-three years. He was inducted into the Cheyenne Frontier Days™ Hall of Fame in 2004. For more than forty years, his voice rang out at Frontier Park when he opened the annual rodeo by singing the National Anthem.

Bill's voice was also heard as a member of the Capital Chorale for many years. He served as a past president and member of the Cheyenne Concert Association and was a member of the choir and an elder at the First Presbyterian Church in Cheyenne.

William "Bill" Dubois III was a well-known teacher and actor in Cheyenne. He is shown here, on the left, receiving a check from Mr. Stephauson of the Recreation Commission for the restoration of the Atlas Theater in 1980. *Wyoming State Archives, Department of State Parks and Cultural Resources.*

Dubois not only served the city of Cheyenne, but he was active throughout Wyoming. He served the State Commission for State Parks and Cultural Resources and the board of advisors from the American Heritage Center at the University of Wyoming, and he was a bill reader in the Wyoming state legislature for sixteen years. And he was on the board of trustees for Laramie County Community College. He was also a member of the board of directors for the Cheyenne Regional Medical Center, a board member of the historic governor's mansion and a member of the board for the Cheyenne Depot Museum.

Bill was a supporter of the Cheyenne Little Theatre Players, serving as a board member and president of the group. He was given a life membership to the theater in 1986, an honor that recognized the contributions of his grandfather William Dubois, who had designed the remodeled addition of the Atlas Theatre in 1907.

These grave markers in Lakeview Cemetery honor the lives of William "Robert" Dubois II and Elinor Dubois, the parents of William "Bill" Dubois III, known as "Teacher." *Starley Talbott photograph.*

One of Bill's many contributions to the history of Cheyenne was as one of the coauthors of *The Magic City of the Plains*, which was published in 1965 for Cheyenne's centennial. In 2017, during Cheyenne's sesquicentennial year, Bill was named "Cheyenne's Historical Laureate."

The remarkable life of one of Cheyenne's most prominent historians, William R. "Bill" Dubois, ended on July 17, 2021. He was cremated, but his memory lives on at Lakeview Cemetery, along with those of his numerous famous family members. Bill was honored with a small park dedicated to his many accomplishments at the corner of Randall and Dey Avenues in Cheyenne. The park is officially named the William R. "Bill" Dubois Memorial Park.

# 6

# AMOS BARBER

## *Wyoming's Cowboy Doctor*

octor Amos Barber arrived in Wyoming in 1885 at the age of twenty-four. He was dispatched to Wyoming to take charge of the Fort Fetterman Hospital. The fort had been abandoned by the United States Army in 1882 and then operated as a private enterprise named the Fetterman Hospital Association. Funded by local ranchers, this association was America's first healthcare cooperative.

The association paid Dr. Barber one hundred dollars a month. He quickly established a reputation as an excellent doctor and surgeon serving the widespread community surrounding the fort. In his first year, he treated 149 patients, including a significant number of cowboys with broken bones.

Barber became a specialist in treating gunshot wounds and rattlesnake bites. Of particular importance was his treatment for rattlesnake bites. Through his considerable experience, he pioneered the use of permanganate of potassium to counteract the snake's venom. This was one of the earliest effective treatments for the injury, and his treatment became commonplace throughout the Rocky Mountain region. Locals also came to rely on the young man who never failed to respond to a call. In one instance, he rode a horse for more than fifty miles to an isolated ranch where the rancher's daughter was dying from a rattlesnake attack. Since Dr. Barber could not treat her on-site, he carried her back to Fort Fetterman, where he used his treatment to save her life.

Amos W. Barber was born in Bucks County, Pennsylvania, on April 26, 1861. Raised and educated in his hometown of Doylestown, he entered the

Doylestown Seminary after completing his public education and then attended the University of Pennsylvania, receiving a medical degree with honor in 1883. For the next two years, he served as a resident physician at the University Hospital, the Children's Hospital of Pennsylvania, and the Pennsylvania Hospital and as a substitute physician at the Episcopal Hospital.

Following his tenure at Fort Fetterman, Dr. Barber moved his practice to the nearby town of Douglas shortly after the railroad town was founded there in 1888. The hospital was also relocated to Douglas.

With the coming of statehood in 1890, Barber became involved in politics. He won the election to become the state's first secretary of state. He served in that role

Amos Barber, the acting governor of Wyoming from November 24, 1890, to January 2, 1893. *Wyoming State Archives, Department of State Parks and Cultural Resources.*

for only a couple of months before Governor Francis E. Warren resigned. Barber then became the acting governor and was the youngest man to ever hold that office at the age of twenty-nine. He served as acting governor until the elections of 1892. Newspapers at the time wondered if he was up to the task. Even Douglas papers cautioned the new governor to beware of the intentions of his compatriots in the legislature.

Barber found himself embroiled in the aftermath of the Johnson County War in 1892 (a conflict between Wyoming's cattle barons and smaller ranchers in Northern Wyoming). Historians have speculated but have not proved that Governor Barber was aware of the invaders' plans but did nothing to stop them. When it was announced that the invaders were in danger of being wiped out at the T.A. Ranch, Barber appealed to the president to dispatch troops from Fort McKinney to suppress what he called an "insurrection." President Harrison did so, and the Johnson County War was brought to an end with the intervention of the United States Army.

When Dr. John E. Osborne was elected as Wyoming's new governor in 1892, Barber reverted to his title of secretary of state. One month later, he married Miss Meno Kent, and the couple eventually became parents to two children. Barber returned to civilian life and resumed his medical practice, this time in Cheyenne.

Though Barber did not return to politics, he still took part in the inaugurations of all the future governors of Wyoming during his lifetime. He often organized and hosted arrangements for inauguration celebrations. Barber was frequently offered the position of honor at banquets, though he usually declined, saying he would rather serve than be honored. He was friends with many, including Wyoming senator John B. Kendrick, E.H. Harriman (president of the Union Pacific Railroad) and President Theodore Roosevelt. Barber spent all night preparing a dinner reception for President Roosevelt when he visited Cheyenne in 1908. He declined to sit as a guest at the table, instead watching from the sidelines to make sure everything went smoothly.

In 1898, Barber joined the United States Army to become a surgeon during the Spanish American War. He returned to his practice in Cheyenne after the conflict and entered practice with Doctor G.F. Fox. Barber became known as one of the best surgeons between Omaha and Salt Lake City and was given credit for delivering hundreds of babies. In 1903, he became the secretary for the State Board of Health and took part in an effort to combat an outbreak of smallpox in the Cheyenne area in November that year. In

The memorial marker for Amos Barber in Lakeview Cemetery. *Starley Talbott photograph.*

1909, as secretary of the Red Cross, he helped organize the local effort to raise funds and support for the victims of the San Francisco earthquake.

In a tribute to his care and character, one of his patients, Vivian Henderson, paid tribute to Dr. Barber with the following words:

> *The declining days of the aged have been made happier and the discomforts of little patients have been lessened by the sunshine that Dr. Barber always carried on his daily rounds. Though never grave or serious in the sick room, he studied all cases carefully and his vigilance made him forgetful of self and the need of rest. Fathers and mothers in mansion and humble cottage remember how, in times of crisis, he has watched patiently all through the night vanquishing disease, leaving at daybreak with scant time for sleep, before taking up the duties of a busy day. He never wearied, his cheer never failed, his humor never dulled.*

In February 1915, Barber became extremely ill and diagnosed his own condition as being very serious. It was never relayed what his malady was, but he felt compelled to seek help at the Mayo Brothers Clinic in Rochester, Minnesota, in March. An extensive surgery offered hope, and the newspapers followed his recovery closely. Unfortunately, Barber succumbed to his malady on May 18, 1915, and was buried in Cheyenne's Lakeview Cemetery.

# 7

# WILLIAM ALFORD RICHARDS

## *Rough Mountains and Deep Canyons*

**W**illiam Alford Richards worked his way westward from Wisconsin, to Illinois, to Nebraska and finally to Wyoming. In Nebraska, he joined a government surveying party, and eventually, he did some survey work in Wyoming. After moving farther west for a time, Richards returned to Wyoming in 1884 and established a ranch in northern Wyoming.

Richards was born on March 9, 1849, to his parents, Truman and Eleanor Swinnerton Richards, in Hazel Green, Wisconsin. He grew up on the family farm and attended the excellent public schools of Grant County. In 1863, he left home to follow his brother Alonzo into the Union Army as part of the Army of the Potomac, where he served as an ambulance driver. He had wished to be a soldier, but officers thought he was too young for the role, being only fourteen at the time.

After the war, Richards moved to Galena, Illinois, and attended high school there. Two years later, he returned to his home county and began to teach. Later, he returned to Illinois to teach in Jo Davis County.

As a young man, Richards yearned to head west and experience the frontier. In 1868, he found employment as a farmer at the home of Ulysses S. Grant in Galena, Illinois. In the spring of 1869, he went to Omaha, Nebraska, to join a government surveying party. The next year, he sought to gain a contract to conduct his own surveys. He approached General Livingston, the surveyor general of Nebraska, with a note from a special benefactor who had taken interest in his affairs. It read:

*Executive Mansion, Washington D.C.,*
*May 17, 1870.*

*Dear Sir:*
*Permit me to recommend to your favorable notice Mr. Wm. A. Richards,*
*now a citizen of Nebraska. Mr. Richards is a worthy, industrious young*
*man, and well qualified for such work as our surveyor generals in new*
*states and territories have to give. He is a young man who would highly*
*appreciate any opportunity given him to make a fair start in the world.*

*With Great Respect,*
*Your Obedient Servant,*
*U.S. Grant*
*To Gen. Livingston, Surveyor General of Nebraska*

Richards got the job and continued to work on Nebraska surveys until 1873. When not in the field, Richards did editorial work for local newspapers and was a money order and registry clerk for the Omaha Post Office. He also studied law in the office of Judge Wakely, where he qualified in the law but was not admitted to the bar.

In 1873 and into early 1874, William and his brother Alonzo surveyed the southern and western borders of Wyoming Territory. In May 1874, the brothers began their survey of the western border. William kept a diary during the summer months of the trek to the north that included many difficulties. He wrote on July 10:

*Fourteen hours without eating, and climbing the worst kind of mountains,*
*inclines one to relish his supper of bean soup, ham, coffee and bread melted*
*before our appetites like dew before the sun.*

On August 26, William and others set the monument for the northern terminus 278 miles from the southwest corner.

William moved to California later in 1874 to undertake surveys in that state, and he secured a position as the surveyor of Santa Clara County. In addition to his survey work, Richards took up wheat farming near San Jose. He married Harriet Hunt of Oakland on December 28, 1874. The couple eventually became the parents of four daughters.

After several years, due to complications of tuberculosis, William was compelled to travel to Colorado for his health in 1881. He again took up survey work, this time employed on public surveys as a civil engineer on the Denver and Rio Grande Railway. In 1883, Richards served for a time as a surveyor in El Paso County and the city engineer of Colorado Springs.

In 1884, he decided to move to Wyoming and landed in the Big Horn Basin in Johnson County. He entered the state near Rawlins, and while his family rode along in a wagon, he drove his horses and cattle to their new home at Red Bank.

He was intensely interested in irrigation, the reclamation of arid lands and raising livestock. He dug a twenty-mile ditch to irrigate his twenty-thousand-acre ranch with water from the Big Horn River. In 1886, he was elected county commissioner for Johnson County and began moving his family from his ranch to Buffalo to spend the winters. He did not always do this, which caused problems for him, especially in the spring of 1888. On April 7, the *Big Horn Sentinel* published one of his most harrowing misadventures:

*Traveling Under Difficulties; The Pleasure of Being a County Official in Some Parts of Wyoming*

*To one who thinks there is pleasure in making the trip across the Big Horn Mountains at this season of the year from the No Wood country, an experience such as that gone through by County Commissioner Richards a few days ago would certainly convince him to the contrary.*

*Mr. Richards resides on the Big Horn River with his family, where he is engaged in ranching and stock growing. The inconvenience of reaching the county seat in the winter season, Mr. Richards was fully aware of, but thinking his presence might be required on matters pertaining to the interest of the county he left his home on horseback last Tuesday morning, booked for Buffalo, accompanied by one of his men with a pack-horse loaded with the necessary provisions and bedding for camping out, if necessary.*

*The party rapidly covered the distance to the mountains by the morning's ride, but about noon they encountered snow of a considerable depth, and the nearer they approached the top of the "divide" the more apparent did it become that the abandonment of the trip on horseback, at least, was necessary. This being done, Mr. Richards sent his companion back to the ranch with the horses, after arming himself with a pair of snowshoes and a scanty supply of provisions (which consisted of a part of a loaf of bread), and made tracks toward Buffalo. His progress on the trip was not as rapid as he anticipated, for no sooner had he lost sight of his companion than he found that he was to encounter a "chinook," and with the wind blowing at a terrific speed and the snow thawing traveling was almost impossible.*

*Night finally overtook the traveler before he had quite reached the top of the divide. Mr. Richards concluded to make the best of the situation and finding the most suitable spot, he drove his stakes for the night at the side of a big pine stump, where he built a fire and rested his weary limbs on top of several feet of snow. The wind kept up at a furious rate all night and with his scant supply of food and a pipe and tobacco the traveler sat up all night, first warming one side, then the other, and reflecting over the bad deeds committed in his past life.*

*Day dawned and the Johnson County commissioner resumed his onward march, first over precipices and then down ravines and picturesque canyons. All day long he tramped faithfully, not knowing where night would again overtake him. About 6 o'clock in the evening a broad valley opened out before him and in looking over the country he discovered that he was on one of the tributaries of Powder River and within a few miles of the Frontier Cattle Company's home ranch. Reaching the ranch Mr. Richards received a kindly welcome, and here he remained two days to rest up from a tiresome and what may be termed a very difficult journey. Being supplied with a saddle horse from the ranch Mr. Richards, on the morning of the second day of his stay there, resumed his journey, arriving in Buffalo Sunday without experiencing any further trouble.*

Harriet Richards became the first postmistress of their portion of the Big Horn Basin in 1888. She oversaw the Billings to Meeteetse stage line, with the post office located at Red Bank.

Richards's expertise in surveying and his membership in the Republican Party gained him notice. On July 20, 1889, President Benjamin Harrison appointed him the surveyor general of Wyoming Territory. It took a while for Richards to get the word, as he was working a roundup at the time. To be close to his duties, he moved his family to Cheyenne, where he retained the position through statehood and continued until 1893.

In 1894, the Richards moved back to Red Bank, but he was not done with politics. The Wyoming Republican Party nominated Richards without dissent to be the next governor. This was motivated by the widely acknowledged skill in which Richards conducted himself as surveyor general. He defeated William H. Holliday of the Democratic Party and Lewis C. Tidball of the People's Party to become the state's fourth governor.

Willian Richards, the governor of Wyoming from 1895 to 1899. *Wyoming State Archives, Department of State Parks and Cultural Resources.*

Members of the Bannock tribe of Natives threatened to invade the state near Jackson Hole from the Fort Hall Reservation in Idaho. They had hunted in Wyoming regardless of state statutes, even when the hunting season was officially closed. Richards was determined to stop them. Several arrests were made, but that did not deter the Natives. A stronger party was dispatched, and in an attempted escape, one Bannock was killed. In retaliation, several hundred of the tribe took a stand near Jackson Hole, joined by members of other tribes. The U.S. Army interceded and dispersed the tribes, convincing them to return to their own reservations.

The incident led to a case over whether Natives could hunt in Wyoming, regardless of statutes. The case was taken to the United States Supreme Court. The decision in *Race Horse v. Wyoming* upheld Richard's position. The suit inspired laws in other states on hunting rights for Natives.

With the outbreak of the Spanish-American War in 1898, Governor Richards was in charge of ensuring Wyoming fulfilled its quota of volunteers. He thought the quota of a battalion with four companies of infantry was excessive for the small population of the state. Even so, he was able to provide enough men from the Wyoming National Guard to organize the unit. When he reported to the War Department that a battalion was ready to serve, he learned that Wyoming was the first state to report that it had fulfilled its obligations. Ultimately, Wyoming contributed five times the men the War Department had asked for.

When Richards's first term was complete in 1898, he declined to be renominated for governor by his party, and he again refused their attempt to get him to run for the U.S. Senate. The reason for this was that he was asked by President McKinley to become the assistant commissioner of the General Land Office. Richards moved to Washington, D.C., in March 1899. While in his position in Washington, his most notable contribution was the opening of the lands of the Kiowa, Comanche, Apache and Wichita Reservations in Oklahoma to settlement in 1901.

When President Roosevelt succeeded President McKinley after his assassination in 1903, Richards offered his resignation. Roosevelt not only refused, but he also elevated Richards to become the commissioner of the General Land Office of the United States. Richards agreed but told the president that he would modify his resignation and stay through 1907, completing eight full years in office. Roosevelt agreed and immediately put him to work. The president placed Richards at the head of a committee, along with F.N. Newell and Gifford Pinchot, to investigate the nation's current land laws and "the use, condition, disposal, and settlement of the public lands." The committee was to investigate what changes were needed in the law to allow the maximum number of settlers to acquire land and build homes on it and to determine the best use of the resources on public lands. The commission was given great latitude to examine the practices of the general and local land offices, the Reclamation Service, the Bureau of Forestry and the Department of Justice.

While Richards's political star was ascending, tragedy visited the Richards family when Harriet died from a heart condition on October 28, 1903. This sad event wasn't the last the Richards family would endure. Richards continued his work in Washington, while his new company, the Red Bank Cattle Company, was in the process of incorporating at the time of his wife's death.

In 1908, as agreed, Richards again resigned. Roosevelt sent him a note expressing his regret:

*My Dear Commissioner Richards,*

*I hereby accept your resignation. Two years ago you told me that you could not stay longer than this date. I told you then how I regretted to have you go. Let me reiterate my assurances of my personal regard for you, and of appreciation for your long and faithful services. For eight years you have given your best ability to the disinterested service of the Government. I thank you for it on behalf of the government, and I extend to you my heartiest good wishes for your future.*

*Sincerely yours,*
*Theodore Roosevelt*

Richards had hoped to finally settle into a quiet retirement back on his ranch at Red Bank where he and his personal friend George B. McClellan ran the new Red Bank Cattle Company, one of the largest cattle companies in the state. Wyoming was glad to have him back, and retirement would wait. Governor Baxter Brooks named him as the inaugural chair of the commissioner of taxation, a position he held from 1909 to 1910. For a time, he was also the president of the Stock Growers Bank of Worland and the Hannover Canal Company in the Big Horn country. He became involved in the establishment of the Colorado Ditch Company and served as president of the Redbank Telephone Company, the oldest private telephone company in Wyoming. The sunset of his life looked to be one of quiet repose and success. Unfortunately, a horror awaited him.

The Red Bank Ranch was to be the scene of the greatest tragic mystery of Richards's lifetime. Richards and Senator McClellan departed on a hunting trip to Jackson Hole, leaving Mrs. McClellan and Richards family on the ranch.

On September 29, 1911, Mrs. McClellan became concerned when she was unable to reach the nearby home of Richards's youngest daughter Edna Jenkins by phone. The young woman had been married in May to Tom Jenkins and seemed happy. When she was unable to make contact for two days, Mrs. McClellan became alarmed and enlisted the aid of two seventeen-year-old girls to ride out to the home to investigate. As the girls approached the Jenkinses' house, they were horrified to see Edna laying dead beneath the tree in the front yard. She was dressed in a nightgown and bath robe, and in her hand was a pistol. A smaller-caliber pistol was found on the ground nearby. She had been shot through the head and through the lungs. Police later entered the house to find Mr. Jenkins dead in his "union suit" on one of the two beds in the house, killed by a bullet through the heart. Early speculation led newspapers to conclude that the couple had gotten into an argument in which Mr. Jenkins had shot Edna before she shot him dead. She then apparently dragged herself outside and died by suicide.

Newspapers were quick to label the tragedy a murder/suicide, but oddities with the crime scene pointed to foul play. The bed on which Mr. Jenkins was found had caught fire. Someone had doused the blaze with water. The circumstances around Edna were also strange. With mortal chest wounds, did she actually make the effort to put out the fire, dress in a bath robe (which was undamaged) and then go outside to shoot herself with her nondominant hand? There were also other bullet holes found in the walls of the bedroom that weren't of the same caliber of either pistol found at the scene.

Suspicion quickly fell on a troubled journalist, Edward T. Payton, who had recently been seen in the area. Formerly a solicitor for the *Denver Republican* newspaper, Payton had been seen in Washakie County (newly founded in 1911), where he was apparently writing an article about the new territory. He had previously suffered from multiple bouts of insanity and had been hospitalized at the Wyoming State Hospital in Evanston several times. While there, he developed great hostility to Dr. Solier, the manager at the state hospital. Some believed he carried a grudge against Richards, who appointed Solier to the hospital, and was bent on vengeance. Locals around Red Branch stated that they had seen Payton in nearby Big Trails, Wyoming, where he was apparently suffering from another bout of insanity. Payton was arrested on October 6, and two other men were taken into custody. One man was O.K. Fullerton, who was a farmhand on the Red Bank Ranch and was rumored to be attracted to Edna. Another was Tom O'Day, a former member of the Hole-in-the-Wall Gang. Further investigation led authorities to conclude that none of the three men could have committed the crime. No other suspects were found, and the case remains unsolved.

After the killings, the Red Bank Ranch lost its appeal to Richards. Under the terrible circumstances there, he was elated to receive a personal invitation from Elwood Mead to join him in Australia as an opportunity for some distraction.

Mead, who was Wyoming's first engineer, had worked for Richards while the latter was governor. Mead had become widely recognized for his irrigation work in Wyoming and had likewise gone to Washington, where he was the chief of investigation and drainage irrigation for the U.S. Department of Agriculture from 1897 to 1907. In 1907, he became the chairman of the State Rivers and Water Supply Commission in Victoria, Australia, and was doing considerable work there to bring water to that parched land. Mead was eager to show what had been accomplished and invited Richards and several other Americans to visit Australia. Richards said he thoroughly enjoyed his visit in a letter to friends in Cheyenne that arrived on July 15. He intended to stay longer than the rest of the party, and he planned to spend the remainder of the year visiting his daughters in Colorado and California. On July 26, Richards died of heart failure in Melbourne.

Richard's body was shipped back across the Pacific and arrived in Cheyenne on August 19. His body lay in state in the chamber of the house of representatives at the state capitol under guard of the noncommissioned officers of the Wyoming National Guard. The casket moved from there to the rotunda of the capitol and then on to Cheyenne Baptist Church for the funeral. Richards was laid to rest beside his wife in Lakeview Cemetery at a ceremony that was attended by a full military escort squadron of the Ninth Cavalry from Fort D.A. Russell.

# 8

# JOSEPH STIMSON

## *Photographer of the West*

The quiet grandeur of Lakeview Cemetery holds the remains of one of the most accomplished photographers of western lore, Joseph E. Stimson. Fortunately for Wyoming and the world, the Wyoming State Archives holds a collection of the bulk of Stimson's photography.

Stimson was born on May 18, 1870, in Virginia. At the age of sixteen, he started a three-year apprenticeship at his cousin's portrait studio in Appleton, Wisconsin. His work at the studio provided him photography skills using both the collodion, or wet-plate, process and the new dry-plate process of making glass plate negatives.

Even though Stimson was not the first photographer to capture the West in photographs, his accomplishments are noteworthy, in that he provided a visual concept of the area during a transitional time in history.

At the age of nineteen, Stimson put down roots in Cheyenne, arriving in 1889, one year ahead of Wyoming statehood. Within a year, Stimson had purchased a studio and equipment on Capitol Avenue. It was an exciting time in Cheyenne, with the coming of statehood, the glory days of the cattle industry and the building of the city. He worked primarily as a studio portrait photographer for the next decade.

One of Stimson's portraits was that of Anna Peterson. A few years later, when Anna was nineteen and Joseph was twenty-three, the couple was married. They lived in an apartment next to the downtown studio for a few years. In 1904, they moved to a house on Twenty-Fifth Street, just north of the capitol.

Joseph Stimson sitting in his Ford, smoking his favorite pipe, circa 1910. *J.E. Stimson Collection, Wyoming State Archives, Department of State Parks and Cultural Resources.*

The same year Joseph and Anna were married, 1894, an opportunity was presented to Joseph by Elwood Mead, Wyoming's state engineer. Mead brought several glass plate negatives to be developed at Stimson's studio. Stimson was astounded at the scenic beauty found in the negatives and accepted Mead's offer to take him to the Big Horn Mountains in northern Wyoming the following summer. After that experience, Stimson is said to have decided to become a scenic photographer. He was subsequently invited to spend time photographing the Teton Mountains, Jackson and the Yellowstone area.

Stimson's scenic photographs caught the attention of a publicist for the Union Pacific Railroad, and in 1901, he was hired by the Union Pacific to document all facets of the railroad. He was encouraged to photograph natural wonders, towns and cities, farms and ranches, irrigation systems, reclamation projects, mines and industry, as well as the tracks, depots, trains and personnel of the Union Pacific.

Because the young photographer had no restrictions from the Union Pacific and a flexible payment plan, he was able to take a wide variety of

The interior of the Joseph Stimson photography studio on Seventeenth Street in Cheyenne in 1906. *J.E. Stimson Collection, Wyoming State Archives, Department of State Parks and Cultural Resources.*

photographs. He was permitted to retain the negatives he produced for the railroad and then reprint and sell the photographs for himself. He was also allowed to work for other entities at the same time, and he was provided free transportation as long as he traveled by train.

During the next twenty years, Stimson photographed each of the major towns along the Union Pacific line and most of the branch lines throughout the area. He traveled back and forth along the railroad's tracks from the Missouri River to the West Coast.

Amid his photographic journey, Stimson was hired to produce hundreds of photographs for display in St. Louis at the Louisiana Purchase Exposition in 1904. He worked on the project for eight months, traveling throughout Wyoming and developing and printing pictures. The prints were hand-colored, a skill that Stimson often employed before the advent of color film. He earned a silver medal for his exhibit. In 1905, a similar exhibit at the Lewis and Clark Exposition in Portland, Oregon, also received a silver medal.

While Stimson continued to travel around Wyoming, taking photographs, he also developed a love of fishing and hunting. One of his favorite fishing

partners was Lem Ellis, the son of Henry Ellis, who had established a candy store in downtown Cheyenne. Lem eventually took over the candy store while he and Joseph continued to enjoy fishing trips throughout Wyoming.

Since Cheyenne was Stimson's hometown and his workplace, his photographic collection contains more images of the city than any other place. He photographed Cheyenne's people, streets, buildings, homes, businesses and churches. He even recorded the city's first Frontier Days celebration in 1897.

*Opposite*: A train photographed by Joseph Stimson. *J.E. Stimson Collection, Wyoming State Archives, Department of State Parks and Cultural Resources.*

*Above*: Lem Ellis (*right*) and Joseph Stimson (*behind the Cream of Wheat box*), preparing for a fishing trip at the Stimson home near the Wyoming State Capitol in 1912. *J.E. Stimson Collection, Wyoming State Archives, Department of State Parks and Cultural Resources.*

Along with his love of photography, nature and fishing, Stimson was active in the social life of Cheyenne. He was a member of the Masonic Lodge and Congregational church and served as a Laramie County commissioner.

In 1933, Stimson moved his photography studio to the basement of his home near the capitol. Unfortunately, many of his early studio portraits were lost after a shelf collapsed and a number of the glass plates were destroyed as they crashed to the floor. He had photographed many local and regional citizens, recording those images on glass plates, and he often hand colored many of his portraits and scenic images.

After the death of his wife, Anna, in 1938, Joseph went into semiretirement, though he remained active. He received orders from all over the world for his photographs and was known to spend much of his time coloring photographs from his file of negatives. He also traveled to Mexico and

Joseph Stimson's marker in Lakeview Cemetery displaying a Wyoming State Flag. *Starley Talbott photograph.*

several states in the United States. He was hired once again in 1948 to travel to Teton and Yellowstone country to obtain additional photographs for the Wyoming Department of Commerce, which later became the Wyoming Travel Commission.

Several individuals and groups were interested in obtaining Stimson's photographic collection of approximately 7,500 glass plates and nitrate negatives spanning half a century of work. Stimson hoped the collection would be retained in the state of Wyoming.

On February 8, 1952, at the age of eighty-two, Joseph Stimson died of a heart attack while visiting family in Connecticut. After his death, the disposition of the bulk of Stimson's photographs was determined, and his heirs received $2,000 for the collection. The collection is now housed at the Wyoming State Archives, Museums and Historical Department, in Cheyenne.

# 9

# HENRY ELLIS AND LEMUEL ELLIS

## *Pioneer Confectioners*

E arly Cheyenne business establishments included a store that is rare to find today. One of those stores was the Ellis Confectionery and Bakery, originally opened on Eddy Street (now Pioneer Avenue) in 1876.

Henry Ellis was born in England on January 30, 1838, and came to the United States when he was ten years old. He lived in Wisconsin for several years and in Denver before settling in Cheyenne in 1868. He gained a reputation as an excellent business operator in the city. His store specialized in baked products, candy, soda pop and ice cream.

The *Cheyenne Daily Leader* proclaimed, "The Ellis Bakeshop is a model of neatness and has won the approval of the community in the shape of a large patronage." The newspaper went on to say that in the summer months, the bakery turned out one thousand loaves of bread every day, along with pies and cakes. Ellis was also considered the finest purveyor of candy throughout the area.

Ellis kept a notebook with some of the recipes from the bakery. He also kept detailed records of purchases made by his customers. Records from March 13 and 14, 1889, show that Mrs. F.E. Warren, the wife of territorial governor Francis Warren, purchased a pound and a half of Jordan almonds for $1.15, and two pounds of candied oranges for $1.50. On May 8, 1891, E.A. Slack, the editor of the *Cheyenne Daily Sun*, purchased a cake for $0.25.

A recipe from the Ellis notebook for molasses cake says that ½ pound of sugar, ¾ pounds of lard, 1 quart of molasses and 11¼ pounds of flour

Lem Ellis posed with his catch of fish during a trip in Wyoming. *J.E. Stimson Collection, Wyoming State Archives, Department of State Parks and Cultural Resources.*

makes eight dozen cakes. The recipe for spice cookies says that 3½ pounds of flour, twelve eggs, 1 pint of molasses, 1¼ pounds of sugar and 1 pound of butter makes thirteen dozen cookies.

Along with the confection and bakery business, the Ellis family operated an ice business with Timothy Dyer. Before refrigeration was available, ice was cut into blocks from Sloans Lake and stored in an icehouse, where customers could purchase a block of ice, the price of which was determined by by the weight of the block.

Henry had married Adelaide Hollister in Wisconsin in 1867. Their son, Lemuel, was born there on August 9, 1868. They moved to Cheyenne later that year, and in the spring of 1869, the couple built a house on East Nineteenth Street. Their daughter, Gertrude, was born in Cheyenne on August 29, 1870.

Young Lemuel Ellis learned to make candy from his father. He later opened his own store on Seventeenth Street known as the Ellis Candy Shop. His store also contained a soda fountain with several varieties of flavored syrup. Henry continued to be associated with his son in the confectionery business until his death on May 15, 1907. Henry's wife, Adelaide, died in 1926.

Lemuel married Mary Lane in October 1899 in Cheyenne. The couple lived in the house Lemuel's father had built on East Nineteenth Street. Lemuel retired from the candy business in 1921. He was active in photography, fishing and hunting. He was a friend of photographer Joseph Stimson, and the two men went on many camping and fishing expeditions throughout Wyoming.

Lemuel Ellis died on March 12, 1949. His wife, Mary Ellis, died on March 15, 1961. They were buried alongside Lemuel's parents at Lakeview Cemetery.

# 10

# CHARLES BURTON "C.B." IRWIN

## *Wild West Showman*

Charles Burton Irwin, or "C.B." as he liked to be called, knew horses well from an early age and was an excellent rider. He enjoyed showing off his riding skills to all who would watch and would also be quick to demonstrate his remarkable athletic ability as a sprinter when the opportunity arose. Many of his friends recalled that he was always ready for "a frolic, a foot race, or a fist fight."

Irwin was born on August 14, 1875, in Chillicothe, Missouri. From a very young age, he learned his father's trades as a blacksmith and a horse trader. He also worked hard as he followed his father from farm to farm in his youth. While on his many travels, he met and later married Etta May McGukin in January 1894. Their first child, Floyd, was born in April 1895.

In 1896, the entire Irwin clan, consisting of C.B.'s new family, his father, two brothers and a married sister, moved to Colorado Springs, where the family set up a blacksmith's shop. While in Colorado, C.B.'s daughters, Joella and Pauline, were born. In 1899, C.B. and Etta moved their growing family north to Wyoming, where they established a homestead on Horse Creek, north of Cheyenne. He was also hired by C.J. Hysham and Company to serve as foreman on a project to move Wyoming cattle north to Fort Yates, North Dakota, to help feed Natives on the reservation there. Irwin made several friendships among the Sioux tribe, which would prove to be very beneficial.

In 1900, C.B. returned to Cheyenne and was hired on with the Warren Livestock Company as a blacksmith. He met and befriended Warren's brand-new son-in-law, Captain John J. "Blackjack" Pershing. Irwin also worked for various other ranchers in the area and became friends with several of the ranch hands. One of these friendships led to his ownership of a famous horse.

One of Wyoming's most beloved characters is a horse that was born on the Frank Foss ranch near Chugwater in 1896. In 1899, Foss sold the horse to the Swan Land and Cattle Company, whose cowboys tried unsuccessfully to break him to ride. When the hands on the Swan Company's Two Bar Ranch castrated the horse, he hit his head on the ground and broke his nose. The cowboys named him Steamboat, because as a result of the accident, he breathed with a whistling sound. In 1901, the horse was sold to John Coble for his ranch near Bosler.

Coble revered good horses and kept several excellent animals on his ranch. He also kept some ferocious animals for use as bucking stock at the new Cheyenne Frontier Days™ celebration. The ferocious young horse Steamboat was jet-black with three white socks. The young animal was just at the beginning of his career, and C.B. Irwin would become intimately involved in his future fame.

Irwin also became friends with another hired hand, Tom Horn. Horn eventually gave C.B. one of his rifles, a 30/30 Winchester that stayed in the family for over one hundred years. When Horn was put on trial for the murder of Willie Nickell in 1902, C.B. was an ardent defender of his friend's innocence. John Coble funded Horn's defense to no avail, and when Horn went to the gallows, C.B. and his brother Frank sang the song "Life's Railway to Heaven" just before the trapdoor swung open.

The cost of the trial was high, and Coble decided to sell off his bucking string. He sold Steamboat to the Cheyenne Elks Club. Not knowing what to do with this terrible creature, the Elks put him up for auction, and C.B. quickly purchased the animal. Steamboat, along with another ferocious bucker, Teddy Roosevelt, became the core of what would become Irwin's lifelong passion—being a stock contractor and showman.

Irwin's hard work and gregarious nature opened many doors for him. A consummate businessman, he used every opportunity to make money and purchase land. His homestead, now known as the Y6, eventually grew to encompass twenty-three thousand acres. While his work with the ranch continued, C.B. moved his family and his new daughter, Frances, to a permanent home in Cheyenne in 1903.

Upon moving to Cheyenne, C.B. secured another career as a rail agent, first for the moving of livestock and then for general purposes, for the Union

Pacific Railroad. In this new profession, C.B. pioneered the concept of "stock contractors." Beginning in 1903, he was able to take Steamboat and other horses from rodeo to rodeo using the railroad as a means of transportation. This in itself would be enough to fill a year for a busy man, but 1903 had a special occasion that demanded all the effort Irwin could muster. In May, President Teddy Roosevelt visited Cheyenne. A special celebration of Cheyenne Frontier Days™ was organized and C.B., along with his friend and partner Charlie Hirsig, provided all the stock used. Irwin and Hirsig worked together as stock contractors until 1912.

The year 1906 proved to be a remarkable one for the Irwin family during Cheyenne Frontier Days™. Steamboat, the heretofore famous unrideable horse, was finally defeated by Dick Stanley. The horse was still the most sought-after animal in rodeos across the nation. C.B., despite his growing size due to a thyroid condition, proved that he was a world-class competitor when he won the World's Championship Steer Roping contest, establishing a record of 38$\frac{1}{5}$ seconds. In that era, the steer was given a head start of one hundred feet. C.B.'s record would stand for the next six years, and then, it was only defeated when the lead distance for the steer was reduced to sixty feet.

Charles B. Irwin was a champion steer roper and won the Cheyenne title atop his horse Custer in 1906. *J.E. Stimson Collection, Wyoming State Archives, Department of State Parks and Cultural Resources.*

Irwin's son Floyd also performed well in the 1906 rodeo. Following in his father's footsteps, Floyd began to show remarkable roping and trick riding skills that impressed the crowd. This was also the first year of the Denver Post Ladies' Relay Race. This exciting contest among the cowgirls required them to mount one of three saddled horses held by an assistant. At the word "go," the cowgirls would spur their horses at full speed once around the track, where they were then required to leave their original horse and get on a second mount, race around the track again and then mount a third animal for the last leg. At all times, there was supposed to be only one "assistant" to handle all three horses. C.B. and others helped his daughter Joella, a clear violation of the rules, and after loud protests from the crowd, the race was rerun. Joella didn't win, but she eventually became one of the great champions of the event, winning in 1911 and 1915.

In 1908, Cheyenne Frontier Days™ (CFD) moved to its current location, where a larger arena and grandstand were built. C.B. and his family built their own barn, corral and cookhouse nearby. The cookhouse, built to feed the help for CFD and run by Etta, became famous for not turning down anyone who came by for a meal. Several people called on the Irwins at the cookhouse, and C.B. befriended them all. Some of the guests included humorist Will Rogers, actor Douglas Fairbanks, tycoon Baron Guy de Rothschild and renowned future artist Charlie Russell.

The Wyoming Fair Board also elected Irwin to represent the state at the national convention of fair boards in 1908. While there, C.B. generated the concept of the *Irwin Brothers' Cheyenne Frontier Days Wild West Show* and his life as a showman began. Upon his return, C.B. enlisted his brother Frank to join the new venture. C.B.'s wife and children all became involved as well. C.B. would demonstrate his remarkable roping skills and act as the arena director and stock contractor, while his son Floyd would do fancy trick riding. C.B.'s daughters would do relay races, and little Frances would do rope tricks on the ground and on the back of a tamed Texas longhorn steer.

Irwin's friendship with the Sioux paid dividends at this time, as fifty of them joined his troupe. The transportation of this large group would be provided, conveniently enough, by the Union Pacific Railroad. With used railroad cars purchased from the Ringling Brothers Circus, the show toured the country and was popular from its creation until 1917. The only problem the new company faced was when it was sued by Cheyenne Frontier Days™ for the use of its name in 1912. The family dropped the CFD title and remained good friends and supporters of the event thereafter.

Kelli Cook portrayed Frances Irwin during the Lakeview Living History Walk in 2022. *Starley Talbott photograph.*

As the Irwin family's entertainment business grew, other family members, including nieces, nephews, sisters-in-law and others, joined the cast. Others who joined the troupe included Jane Bernoudy, the first great cowgirl trick roper, former *Buffalo Bill Wild West Show* cowgirl Marie Danks, sharpshooter Captain Hardy and former CFD champions Charlie McKinley, Hugh Clark and Clayton Danks. Subsequently, all of this talent was also made available to Cheyenne Frontier Days™ for each of its annual celebrations. Through it all, the people of the *Irwin Brothers' Wild West Show* became famous for their skill, with many family and staff members winning numerous championships at rodeos around the country. With their considerable experience of putting on a show and conducting stock contracting for rodeos, the company also produced major rodeo events around the country. The family occasionally put together the shows for the Pendleton Roundup, the Winnipeg Stampede and, in 1916, provided livestock for the New York Stampede.

When the twentieth century entered its second decade, C.B. had remarkable successes and deep tragedies. In 1914, the legendary Steamboat cut his leg on a fence after a performance in Salt Lake City. By the time the animal had been returned to Cheyenne, blood poisoning had set in, and the famed animal was doomed. There are many accounts of what happened to Steamboat after the accident. What is known is that C.B. had to put his beloved horse down, and for this purpose, he used the rifle that Tom Horn had given to him several years before. Where the famed animal's body was buried is uncertain, but it is widely believed to have been buried at Frontier Park, though many believe that is not true.

In 1915, C.B. used his influence as a stock contractor and producer for Cheyenne Frontier Days™ to help quell protests by the American Humane Society, who thought the sport of rodeo was too rough on animals. A committee was formed that included Harry Brannan, the 1904 CFD saddle bronc champion, to discuss a series of rules that would guide the events at the rodeo for the betterment of man and beast alike. The presentation of their recommendations was carefully considered by the Humane Society and the CFD Committee. The result was the creation of the Cheyenne Rules, which still guide the sport of worldwide rodeo today.

On a more tragic note, Frances Warren Pershing, the wife of General John J. Pershing, perished in a fire at the Presidio in San Francisco, along with three of her children. The grieved General Pershing, who was on assignment chasing Pancho Villa, called on his friend C.B. to arrange the return of their bodies to Cheyenne. C.B. solemnly took on the responsibility and escorted the remains to Cheyenne for services and burial.

On February 9, 1916, a train robbery near Medicine Bow, Wyoming, set Irwin, as rail agent for the Union Pacific, off in pursuit of the robber. The "white masked bandit," who had held up the train and escaped with $52.35, was Bill Carlisle, a young man who was down on his luck and committed the deed out of desperation. Irwin nearly caught Carlisle a few days later.

The original posse, including Irwin, failed to catch the young robber, and Irwin went to Green River to purchase a ticket to return home. While he was talking to the ticket agent, the agent told Irwin that there was another customer behind him. Irwin stepped aside, and a young man came forward and bought a ticket for Wheatland. The man, after he purchased the ticket, hurriedly turned away from the counter. At that, Irwin grasped the man's shoulder and informed the noticeably nervous fellow that he had forgotten his change. The man took his change and left. Thinking nothing of it, C.B. returned to his conversation after the stranger disappeared. That stranger, it turned out, was Bill Carlisle. Carlisle had recognized C.B. from Cheyenne and thought that when Irwin grasped his shoulder, he was caught. Irwin had no idea at the time that his quarry was literally within his grasp.

The manhunt for Carlisle continued, and C.B. found himself traveling the state, following leads from Casper to Green River. Carlisle robbed two more trains before his luck finally ran out. Sheriff Rubie Rivera captured him on April 22 north of Walcott. Two days later, Carlisle was turned over to C.B., who took the robber's confession. There was no mention that Carlisle and Irwin had already crossed paths. That revelation came many years later during a recorded interview with Carlisle at the University of Wyoming, prior to his death in 1964. In 1919, Carlisle escaped from prison, robbed another train and was captured again. The manhunt, this time, was managed by the State of Wyoming instead of the Union Pacific. C.B. interviewed Carlisle after his capture. The two men talked about Carlisle's escape, his plans to get away and the robbery of the train, and true to his nature, C.B. and Bill Carlisle were on a first name basis.

Another tragedy to strike the family was the death of Floyd Irwin just prior to the Cheyenne Frontier Days™ in 1917. The accident occurred when Floyd was practicing his steer roping with other cowboys prior to the event. In one practice throw, Floyd threw his rope at a steer, thought he missed and turned his horse away as a result. But the throw did catch one of the animal's legs, and when the rope unexpectedly snapped tight, the startled horse threw his head back, impacting Floyd's own. The blow crushed his skull and killed the young man instantly.

Floyd Irwin's funeral included a large parade of cowboys, Sioux and soldiers from Fort Russell in one of the greatest funerary spectacles the city had ever witnessed. Floyd's death prompted the bereaved C.B. to disband the *Irwin Brothers' Wild West Show*. He lent his voice to announce that year's Cheyenne Frontier Days™ celebration and allowed himself to grieve afterward.

The Floyd Irwin grave marker. *Starley Talbott photograph.*

After Floyd's shocking death and the conclusion of the *Irwin Brothers' Wild West Show*, C.B. threw himself into his lifelong passion of horse racing. For the remainder of his life, he raised and trained horses on his Y6 Ranch to challenge the best in the country. His summers were always dedicated to Cheyenne Frontier Days™ and other rodeos around the nation and Canada, to which he provided stock. The rest of the year, particularly in the spring and fall, he would race horses throughout the east. In the winter, he raced in Tijuana, Mexico. Eventually, he and his family built a winter home in San Ysidro, California. In 1923 alone, Irwin's string of horses provided 147 winners, the highest record up to that time. In 1927, C.B. was made a special representative of the Union Pacific Railroad. His duties were to run the various trains that were bringing large numbers of spectators from across the country to the many horse races served by the railroad.

Whether it was in service to the sport of rodeo or to horse racing, few people could match what C.B. Irwin did for either sport. He was also known for his boundless charity, and he frequently got into financial trouble feeding the numerous people who showed up at his cookhouse. C.B. also did everything he could for any cowboy he met who was down on his luck, regardless of whether he was met on the rodeo circuit or on the racetrack.

It wasn't until after C.B. died that his family discovered his scale when they found copious letters and notes of thanks from hundreds of people who owed C.B. appreciation for help securing food, work and even education.

From almost any direction one approached C.B., it was obvious that he was a special individual. He made and kept friends across the country. All were dismayed when they heard that he was in a terrible car crash on May 22, 1934. His coupe, driven by his son-in-law Claude Sawyer, suffered a blowout on the road between Torrington and Cheyenne, about ten miles north of the capital city. The vehicle left the road, went into a ditch and flipped. C.B. was crushed between the seat and the dashboard; he was pried loose with a fencepost by P.T. Lehmer of Torrington, who witnessed the crash. Several men helped load C.B. into an ambulance to Cheyenne, where it was hoped he and Claude would recover. Claude survived, but despite the best efforts of his doctors to save his life, C.B. died on May 23 as a consequence of his internal injuries.

Heartfelt sympathy poured in from across the nation, with expressions of universal grief and shock. The junior high auditorium was reserved for the service, which included more than one thousand mourners. Eight men, all cowboys, served as pallbearers to move the casket that was specially made for C.B.'s body (he weighed nearly five hundred pounds at his death). Honorary pallbearers included actors, humorists, generals, railroad presidents, tycoons and people from all other walks of life. Among them were General John J. "Blackjack" Pershing, Will Rogers, T. Joe Cahill, Charles Hirsig, Warren Richardson, William F. Jeffers, George Brandies, Fred Stone and many others. After the ceremony, a mile-long cortege escorted C.B. to his final resting place in Lakeview Cemetery.

Cheyenne Frontier Days™ paid tribute to its greatest champion and friend that year when Ed Storey, general chairman of Cheyenne Frontier Days™, read aloud Charles Badger Clark's famous poem "The Cowboy's Prayer" to a respectful crowd in the grandstands. For every annual rodeo since 1934, the poem has been read at the beginning of every Thursday rodeo in memory of the contestants, friends and volunteers who have been lost in the previous year.

Charles Burton Irwin was inducted into the National Cowboy Hall of Fame in 1975 and the first class of the Cheyenne Frontier Days™ Hall of Fame in 2002.

# DeFOREST RICHARDS

## *Champion of Woolgrowers*

Wyoming in the late 1800s saw the glory days of the cattle barons who grazed their herds on vast areas of open rangeland. However, some landowners began bringing sheep to their ranches and farms. In 1888, along came a future Wyoming governor who established a sheep operation and became a champion for the Wyoming sheep industry.

DeForest Richards became Wyoming's fifth governor, serving from January 2, 1899, to April 28, 1903. He traveled a long way and experienced many adventures before his political career blossomed in Wyoming.

Governor Richards was born from a long line of exemplary American men. His maternal grandfather was William Jarvis, a leading member of Massachusetts society who was appointed ambassador to Portugal by President Thomas Jefferson in 1802. It was through his efforts that the first Merino sheep were brought to the United States, giving a tremendous boost to the nation's wool industry.

DeForest was born on August 8, 1846, to Jonas DeForest Richards, a Congregational minister and president of the Ohio Female Seminary at College Hill, New Hampshire, and Harriet Bartlett Richards in Charleston, New Hampshire. His childhood was spent in the common schools of Wethersfield, Vermont, and later at the Kimball Union Academy of Meriden, New Hampshire. Afterward, he attended Andover College for only one year before the family's fortunes took him south into the Reconstruction South.

In 1866, at the age of eighteen, DeForest followed his father to Alabama, where the men bought the Eldorado Place Plantation near Prairie Bluff in Wilcox County at auction. The large plantation contained 2,700 acres, a variety of stock animals and one hundred recently freed Black laborers who were employed for the season. DeForest's interests quickly moved into local politics, and in August 1867, he was elected to the Alabama legislature on the Republican ticket at the age of twenty-one. In 1868, he became the sheriff of Wilcox County and served in that capacity until 1872, when he became the county treasurer. In 1871, he married Elsie J. Ingersoll of Alabama, and the couple would eventually have a boy and a girl.

DeForest Richards, the governor of Wyoming from 1899 to 1903. *Wyoming State Archives, Department of State Parks and Cultural Resources.*

DeForest quit politics for a time and instead poured his effort into running a tannery business. Unfortunately, the business was not successful. Faced with destitution or bankruptcy, Richards decided not to claim bankruptcy and instead worked as a shoemaker to pay off his debts. He learned the trade from an old Black cobbler and then went into business again. Within two years, he had paid off his debt and was actually $1,200 ahead. He established a mercantile in Camden, Alabama, and thrived.

In 1885, Richards desired to go west and try his fortunes. He relocated to Chadron, Nebraska, where he became the president of Chadron National Bank. Chadron proved to be an excellent move for Richards, as he thrived in the area's banking and mercantile industries.

The young banker soon discovered opportunities in nearby Wyoming, where he established the First National Bank in Douglas. DeForest was named president of that firm, and he held that position for the rest of his life.

For the time being, he still resided in Nebraska and was elected the Dawes County treasurer in 1886. He remained in Nebraska until his official duties as treasurer were concluded. He then moved permanently to Douglas in 1888, and there, he continued to pursue the mercantile business, opening branches in Casper and several other communities in the northern part of the territory.

During the next several years, Richard's business ventures expanded and diversified. He became deeply involved in the growing Wyoming sheep industry, becoming president of the Platte Valley Sheep Company. He also established the Lander Transportation Company, which plied many freight routes throughout Wyoming, employing several hundred teams of horses and nearly as many men. The main business of this firm was the transportation of wool to market, and in 1901, the firm moved six million pounds of the commodity.

When the Panic of 1893 descended on the nation, Richards, as president of the Douglas National Bank, was determined not to foreclose against indebted sheepmen. For many years prior to the panic, the bank had made substantial loans to the wool growers in Converse County. Now that the bank's assets were under considerable threat, the directors demanded that Richards call in the debts. Richards knew that doing so would ruin the sheepmen and cause considerable damage to many businesses in Converse County. When he refused, the directors resigned en masse. Despite their revolt, the Douglas National Bank maintained its stability, and Richards never asked the government for help. As a result, the local wool industry and Douglas itself were saved from destitution.

Success in politics continued to follow Richards. In 1890, he was elected mayor of Douglas, a position he held until 1894. He was also in the commission to draft the Wyoming Constitution, and he served as commander of the Wyoming National Guard. In addition to these duties, he became a state senator from 1892 to 1893.

In the contentious aftermath of the Johnson County War (a conflict between the cattle barons and smaller ranchers), the Wyoming senate was in turmoil. One Democratic senator, Fremont County's James Kime, fell seriously ill. Many members of the senate speculated that he had been poisoned, which proved to be true after a medical examination. The senate immediately set up a commission to investigate, with DeForest Richards, Fenimore Chatterton and W.H. Holliday as its members. Two senators were found to have been responsible. One left town, and the other was censured.

Richards and Fenimore Chatterton became friends, and in 1898, they rode together from Casper on a buckboard for 1,500 miles on the campaign trail through north and northwest Wyoming. Richards was unanimously selected as the Republican candidate for governor, and Chatterton, at Richards's urging, accepted the nomination for secretary of state. While on this trip, the two men pledged that if they won their offices, they would work hard to open the lands in the Wind River Reservation north of the Big Wind River to settlement and reclamation.

Richards was elected as Wyoming's fifth governor, and through their efforts, Richards and Chatterton expanded settled land in Wyoming by over one million acres. The towns of Riverton, Shoshoni, Pavillion, Worland, Byron, Cowley, Lovell and Powell were established in these territories.

An ardent Republican, Richards was well respected in the party and had strong support throughout Wyoming. His first few months in office were uneventful, allowing him to travel across the state to look after the state's affairs.

This mild duty was jolted on June 2, 1899, with the announcement that a Union Pacific train had been robbed in Wilcox. The perpetrators were the infamous Hole-in-the-Wall Gang, who used dynamite to blast open a safe and a good portion of the railcar that contained it. This robbery, one of the most celebrated train robberies in American history, touched off a statewide manhunt. Absconding with nearly $50,000, the six men fled into the wilderness. On June 6, a posse led by Converse County sheriff Josiah Hazen tracked three of the bandits to Castle Creek. The outlaws were ready for the lawmen and ambushed the posse, mortally wounding Hazen and making their escape. On June 13, Richards ordered the Buffalo militia to join the manhunt, and two horse-mounted groups from that location scoured the countryside around the Hole-in-the-Wall area to no avail. The War Department promised Richards that troops from Forts Washakie and Yellowstone would also aid in the hunt, but they were equally unsuccessful in bringing the criminals to justice. As it became clear that the villains had escaped, the furor subsided. It would be years before all the suspected perpetrators were brought to justice—and in places widely dispersed outside Wyoming's borders.

In 1901, the murder of Willie Nickell brought statewide outrage and considerable attention to the growing range wars that were breaking out between the cattle and sheep operations. Willie's family owned sheep on their ranch north of Cheyenne. It was speculated that a hired gunman had killed fourteen-year-old Willie Nickell instead of Willie's father. Governor Richards had been wholeheartedly in support of the creation of the Wyoming Wool Growers Association to protect the interests of the wool industry in the state. Alarmed by the growing conflict and eager to put an end to the violence, Richards issued a proclamation on July 25, offering a $500 reward for information that led to the arrest and conviction of the killer. Richards continued to side with the wool growers against attacks by cattlemen and encouraged both sides to drop their misconceptions and work together.

In 1902, the Republican Party of Wyoming again wanted Richards as governor. He was pleased to report that during his administration, the state had been doing very well. The government was well run, with several new facilities being built across the state and expenses actually going down. Large amounts of land were now under irrigation, and Wyoming's credit was in very good condition.

Richards won reelection handily and set about new initiatives for the state. One initiative was to reform the tax laws of Wyoming regarding its mineral wealth. Working in close association with Secretary of State Chatterton, Richards devised new regulations for the taxation of all products that came out of Wyoming's mines. Introduced as the Bill for the Taxation of the Products of Mines in 1903, the new legislation would cover precious metals, salt, coal, petroleum and other natural deposits. The bill passed the house without opposition yet ran into difficulties in the senate.

During this battle, Richards was struck with a severe kidney ailment. For two weeks—and in declining health—Richards remained in his office, working hard to get the bill passed. Eventually, his personal doctor, Amos Barber, insisted that he stop his work and try to recuperate. Despite following the doctor's orders, Richards's health slipped away rapidly. Governor Richards died on April 28, 1903, shortly after the new taxation bill passed.

With his death, Richards became the first governor of the State of Wyoming to die while in office. His passing was universally lamented, and many in Wyoming understood the gravity of the loss of such an able administrator and benefactor of Wyoming's people.

# 12

# WILLIE NICKELL

## *Range War Victim*

Willie Nickell grew up on his family's ranch in Farthing, Wyoming, northwest of Cheyenne, where he was born on May 4, 1887. Willie was the third child of Kels and Mary Nickell, who ranched in the Iron Mountain area of Laramie County.

Kels Nickell established a homestead in the Iron Mountain area in 1885 and built a six-room log cabin and small outbuildings on the property. Most of Wyoming, at that time, was claimed by large cattle companies for grazing purposes. These companies owned the water holes and streams, and they claimed all the land for miles around as theirs by right of prior use, and they did not welcome the intrusion of homesteaders.

Willie lived the typical life of a ranch child, riding horses, raising animals, helping with ranch chores and living "wild and free." The ranchers in the area raised mostly cattle, and Willie's father committed an unforgivable sin by bringing sheep onto his ranch.

Controversy erupted among the ranching neighbors, and the elder Nickell feuded with neighbors about sheep being in cattle country. Fourteen-year-old Willie ended up being the victim of what was called the "Iron Mountain Range War."

On July 18, 1901, young Willie was riding his father's favorite horse while wearing his father's coat and hat. Willie never came home. He was shot and died that day.

According to newspaper reports, Willie left the ranch to go to the railroad station to bring out a sheep herder. When Willie had not returned by the

Willie Nickell on horseback.
*Wyoming State Archives,
Department of State Parks and
Cultural Resources.*

next morning, his father and a visitor went to look for him. They found his body lying face down in the road, a bullet hole through his back. Willie's father took Willie's body back to the ranch and sent a message to the sheriff.

As the investigation into the murder of Willie began, funeral services for the young man were conducted in Cheyenne. The *Cheyenne Leader* published the service information with the following statement:

> *Yesterday afternoon at 3 o'clock at the First Methodist Church the funeral of Will Nickell was held. It was a sad and impressive occasion. To die is hard, but to be cut off just in the bloom of youth, when all nature smiles with gladness, and by hand of a murderer, is the sum of human sorrow for those who are left to mourn the loss of one who has gone.*

It was believed that the killer mistook Willie for his father. Suspicion was cast on a feuding neighbor, but the blame soon turned to Tom Horn, due to his involvement in the range war and prior killings. The Wyoming Stockgrowers Association had hired Tom Horn to clean the range of Wyoming of "rustlers,

Nathan Hurley portrayed Willie Nickell at the Lakeview Cemetery Living History Walk in 2022. *Starley Talbott photograph.*

sheepmen and homesteaders." Kels Nickell had received a warning several times to "take your sheep and get out."

After the murder of Willie Nickell, the county commissioners in Cheyenne hired Deputy United States Marshal Joe LeFors to investigate the crime. LeFors summoned Tom Horn to a meeting in Cheyenne on January 11, 1902, and they met at the marshal's office at 210 West Lincolnway.

Horn had apparently been drinking heavily the night before the meeting. LeFors secreted two people, a stenographer and a witness, behind a locked door. During the meeting, LeFors led Horn into making a series of incriminating remarks about the Nickell killing. The stenographer recorded this statement by Horn: "It was the best shot that I ever made and the dirtiest trick I ever done." The statement was later presented as key evidence in Horn's trial. The confession was given while Horn was drunk, but since he was known as a boaster and a killer, he was deemed the likely murderer of young Willie.

The prosecutors at the trial argued that Horn killed Willie Nickell in order to keep the boy from reporting on his presence in the area. Horn was convicted and hanged in Cheyenne on November 20, 1903. Though, to this day, there is controversy about whether Horn was the killer of Willie.

Kels and Mary Nickell never recovered from the sorrow of Willie's death. They eventually left Iron Mountain and purchased a ranch near Encampment, Wyoming. Kels, Mary and Willie Nickell were buried at Lakeview Cemetery in Cheyenne.

A monument at Lakeview tells the story of a young boy who was murdered at his ranch north of Cheyenne in 1901. A plaque on the north side of the monument briefly explains the story. The east side of the monument lists the names of Willie's parents, Kels and Mary Nickell.

# 13

# FENIMORE CHATTERTON

## *The Courts Ruling Shall Stand*

Fenimore Chatterton moved west in 1878 to become a bookkeeper at Fort Fred Steele. He worked for John Hugus, who operated a trading store at the fort. Hugus soon had the young man involved in many more tasks than just keeping the books.

Before venturing west, Chatterton had an interesting childhood. He was born on July 21, 1860, in Oswego, New York, the son of G.H. Chatterton. Fenimore's father had received an appointment to be the clerk for the United States Census Bureau and moved the family to Washington, D.C.

Fenimore grew up in the busy streets of the nation's capital and had many fond memories. One of his earliest memories was attending the New York Avenue Presbyterian Church. After one of the services, he remembered looking back over his father's shoulders into the eyes of Abraham Lincoln.

In 1865, G.H. Chatterton accepted a position as a minister in Iowa and moved the family to that state. Fenimore recalled that he and his stepmother did not get along, and he was sent back to Washington, D.C., to live with his aunt. His education began at the Columbia College Preparatory School before he moved on to the Franklin Public School and then finally the Millersville State Normal School in Pennsylvania.

At the age of fifteen, Fenimore abandoned the formal classroom setting and was hired on by the law firm owned by Colonel Thompson; there, he began to study the practice of law. He attended sessions of the United States Supreme Court on many occasions, and in 1876, he attempted to become a page there. With no positions available, Fenimore struck out west to find employment.

Chatterton first landed in Chicago and then in Grinnell, Iowa. There, he farmed and worked at a grocery store until he met John W. Hugus, a trader at Fort Fred Steele in Wyoming. After moving to Wyoming, he began a life of adventure in the West.

In one experience, Chatterton remembered bringing a herd of horses from Elk Mountain to Fort Steele in the middle of winter and suffering snow blindness. He recovered from this painful situation and continued with Hugus for several years, learning all aspects of the post trader's business. During that time, he remembered working with Natives, soldiers, railroads workers, ranchers and eventually homesteaders.

By 1881, the country around Fort Steele was beginning to be settled. Hugus began looking for other opportunities, and in 1883, he offered Chatterton the opportunity to buy him out of the business. Chatterton agreed and took over the business himself. He was very successful and grew the store into the largest general store in Carbon County. In 1886, Fort Fred Steele was abandoned by the army, and Chatterton was given the opportunity to move with the garrison to Utah. He declined the offer because he had grown to love his area of Wyoming and was determined to make the best of things. Gradually, the business at the old fort began to decline, and Chatterton looked for a new opportunity.

In 1888, Chatterton laid out the new town of Saratoga on the west side of the North Platte River. The hot springs there inspired him to name the town after the famed resort city of Saratoga, New York. Moving his main store there, Chatterton watched his business expand once again as the community became settled. He likewise became the business manager of the *Platte Valley Register*.

Shortly after his new establishment was underway, Chatterton determined to run for the position of county prosecuting attorney. The Carbon County Republican Party, however, asked him to run for the positions of county prosecuting attorney, probate judge and county treasurer. He was successful in this contest, and he found himself gravitating ever more toward a life of politics. He sold the remainder of his Saratoga business to his partner and became a politician full time in Rawlins. He didn't completely forego private enterprise, however, and in 1889, he took over ownership of the Rawlins Drugstore from Dr. John E. Osborne.

In 1890, the Carbon County Republicans approached Chatterton again, this time asking him to be the first senator for Carbon and Natrona Counties in the new legislature of the State of Wyoming. Natrona County had been authorized during the last territorial legislative session but was yet to be initiated. He once again followed his party's wishes and went to Cheyenne. There, he was part of the difficult process of determining which of the former territory's laws would be retained for use by the new state and which would be amended or repealed.

Chatterton also fulfilled duties on several committees, serving as chairman of the Committee on County Affairs and County Boundaries, and he served on the Sanitary Affairs Committee, the Public Printing, Joint Printing and Public Accounts Committee and the Enrollment Committee. One of his proudest accomplishments during this earliest time in the legislature was that he chaired the committee to create the new great seal of the State of Wyoming. He took a direct hand in designing the seal along with B.H. Beuchner. In that first session, he submitted bills for creating an office of lieutenant governor and to amend and reenact the taxation of railroads and telegraph companies.

Having never attained an official law degree, Chatterton decided to correct this situation in light of his growing involvement with the law of the new state. In 1891, he enrolled at the University of Michigan Law School in Ann Arbor, graduating in 1892. He returned to Rawlins to establish his own law firm. He partnered with David H. Craig, and the two lawyers built a successful practice.

The legislative session of 1893 was one of the most bitter and tumultuous in the state's history. In the aftermath of the Johnson County War, the legislature was bitterly divided between the Democratic and Republican parties. Both sides were acrimonious to the point of open hostility. One of the most vicious disputes was over who would replace U.S. senator Francis E. Warren upon the conclusion of his term. Many believed that the senator was directly involved with the invasion of Johnson County and sought to remove him by all means necessary. As votes were being cast for successors, Senator James Kime of Fremont County became suddenly dangerously ill, and doctors determined that he had been poisoned. Fenimore was on the committee to investigate the crime. James Kime survived, and no one was brought up on charges of attempted murder. Of the two state senators suspected of the crime, one left the state and the other was censured by the senate.

As for the issue of whether to keep Warren in his post, Chatterton was one of the most vocal opponents to his retention, along with DeForest Richards of Douglas. For his opposition to Warren, Chatterton was evermore considered an enemy of Warren, and as a result Chatterton, found several stones placed in the path of his future political career, something Chatterton blamed on the "Warren machine." At the conclusion of Chatterton's second term in the Wyoming legislature in 1894, the Carbon County Republican Convention named him the only candidate for the county prosecuting attorney. He won that position and remained the Carbon County prosecuting attorney for several years.

In 1898, Chatterton was approached by the Wyoming Republican Party to run for secretary of state. On the campaign trail, he met with DeForest Richards, who was running for governor, and the two men developed a close friendship. Together, they campaigned across northern Wyoming and spent considerable time in the undeveloped northwestern portion of the state. Both men agreed that there was significant opportunity to develop the land of the region with suitable investment and labor. Between them, they pledged to work together to bring irrigation to the Big Horn Basin—if they were elected.

When both men did indeed win their elections, they collaborated closely to open portions of the north Wind River Reservation to development and settlement and would eventually open 12,096 square miles of land and help initiate the settlement of Riverton, Shoshoni, Pavillion, Worland, Byron, Cowley, Lovell, Garland and Powell.

Of particular interest to Chatterton was the land that was now becoming available thanks to the Carey Land Act of 1894. The act allowed the federal government to grant up to one million acres of land to arid western states to be irrigated by private companies, which would make money by selling water to settlers on 160-acre tracts. To take full advantage of the opportunities created by these circumstances, Chatterton initiated the Eden Project and the Riverton Project, both of which would bring water to the arid lands around the new settlement of Riverton. To aid in the development of the area, Richards and Chatterton engaged the Mormons to take over the irrigation project in the basin area (including the Sidon Canal) to build a highway between Cody and Yellowstone National Park. They also engaged the Burlington Northern Railroad to build south from Montana to Cody in 1900.

Chatterton had some previous railroad experience that helped bring railroads to northwestern Wyoming. In 1899, he and several other investors created the Wyoming Southern Railroad, which ran between Saratoga and the site of Fort Fred Steele. While they were planning the road, Chatterton, as secretary of the company, secured the interest of the Union Pacific Railroad in the project. The larger company decided to absorb the new line into its system and pay $2 million toward its construction. For the first five years after its completion, the Wyoming Southern Railway operated on its own accord and became part of the Union Pacific Railroad thereafter.

Fenimore Chatterton, the acting governor of Wyoming from April 28, 1903, to January 2, 1905. *J.E. Stimson Collection, Wyoming State Archives, Department of State Parks and Cultural Resources.*

Until this time, Fenimore remained a dedicated bachelor, spending more time on his business and law obligations than on romance. This practice came to an end on October 25, 1900, when he married Stella Wyland in a private ceremony in Des Moines, Iowa. She had previously been a schoolteacher in Rawlins, where the two met. They returned to Chatterton's home in Cheyenne. They had two daughters, Eleanor, born in 1901, and Constance, born in 1904.

For the next two years, Secretary of State Chatterton looked on with satisfaction as the Big Horn Basin country grew and developed. His working relationship with Governor DeForest Richards remained strong, and in the 1902 elections, both men held onto their offices.

In 1903, the two men collaborated on a bill to tax all the extractive products produced by Wyoming's mines for the benefit of the state. Chatterton drafted the bill, and together, both men were able to sail its approval through the Wyoming House. The Wyoming Senate, however, proved to be more contentious. Chatterton and Richards worked closely to convince and cajole a majority to finally approve the bill before the conclusion of the legislative session.

Unfortunately, Governor Richards, who had become critically ill with the inflammation of his kidneys, died shortly thereafter. Since the Wyoming legislature hadn't passed Chatterton's proposed amendment to the Wyoming Constitution, creating the position of lieutenant governor, it fell to Chatterton to assume the role of acting governor of the State of Wyoming until the next election in 1904. It is a testament to the close relationship between the two men that all of Richards' staff remained to support Chatterton. There were several positions in the state government that shifted in the absence of Governor Richards. Chatterton had no small difficulty putting his own choices in place, as he found constant opposition from members of what he called the "Warren machine."

Despite the political battles, there were other incidents of considerable interest that required Chatterton's attention. First was the appearance of

President Teddy Roosevelt in Wyoming. The president, who had assumed the position of head of state after the assassination of President McKinley, accepted Chatterton's invitation to give the Memorial Day address in Cheyenne in May 1903. Roosevelt happily agreed, and this touched off one of the famous excursions of a president through the state. Leaving his train at Laramie on May 30, Roosevelt and an entourage of dignitaries, including Francis E. Warren and Joe LeFors, rode over the continental divide on horseback to Cheyenne. Chatterton met the president on horseback at Fort D.A. Russell and officially welcomed him to Wyoming. The visit lasted several days and included an impromptu rendition of Cheyenne Frontier Days™, specifically put on for the president.

The next occasion in which Governor Chatterton had to engage with the Roosevelt administration was not so pleasant. In September 1903, Chatterton joined the Wyoming Industrial Convention in opposition to the Forestry Grazing Rule put in place by Gifford Pinchot, Roosevelt's secretary of the interior and personal friend. Pinchot's rule would ban cattle grazing within federal timberlands unless the cattlemen lived immediately adjacent to them. The policy would also ban grazing in prime areas in valleys and nearby plains in the forest reserves. Chatterton realized that these were important sources of summertime feeding thanks to their constant supply of fresh grass and water. Chatterton cornered Pinchot on two separate public occasions, forcing the official to defend his policies in front of Wyoming businessmen and county officials. While Pinchot was not particularly happy about these incidents, it reinforced Chatterton's own strong opinion that Wyoming should be consulted and have its rights considered in relation to any natural resources on federal land within the state boundaries.

Chatterton found himself under intense public scrutiny in another incident that year. In November 1903, the Wyoming Supreme Court determined that Tom Horn's conviction for the murder of Willie Nickell should stand. The court found no evidence that the lower courts had acted inappropriately and that his sentence to be executed by hanging should stand. Many powerful people in Wyoming felt that the trial had been deeply flawed and were demanding, if the conviction could not be overturned, that the sentence be commuted to life in prison instead of death. As an experienced attorney himself, Chatterton decided to hear the details of the case and had both the prosecution and defense present their positions to him. When the defense attempted to submit new evidence, he dismissed it. He believed that if the defense had this information during the trial, they should have used it. While he was debating the issue, he received several death threats and ominous visits by private citizens. The latter promised to unseat him in the next election and said they would raise money to do so should he not rule in Horn's favor. Nonetheless, Chatterton was determined to allow the court's ruling to stand, and Horn went to the gallows. Because of the obvious potential for violence, Chatterton called on the local militia to be on hand to keep order during the execution.

Prior to the 1904 election, Chatterton met his match. Forces unleashed by his decision to support the execution of Horn may have played a part in his downfall. He believed that the "Warren machine" was out for vengeance and arrayed forces against him that would oust him from the governor's chair. The Wyoming Republican Convention nominated Bryant B. Brooks instead of Chatterton to be its choice for Wyoming's governor. Denied the opportunity to run for office, Chatterton surrendered his seat to the new governor elect in 1905.

Stung and embittered by his political loss, Chatterton abandoned Cheyenne and undertook new endeavors. From 1905 to 1930, Chatterton lived in Wyoming's northwest, where he worked on the continuing development of that portion of the state. With the backing of Chicago financiers, he founded the Wyoming Central Irrigation Company to manage newly opened lands north of the Wind River Reservation. In 1906, he surveyed and laid out the Town of Riverton and contracted the construction of a canal to open fifteen thousand acres north of the town for new settlement. Chatterton established a farm near Riverton, where he could manage the company and safeguard the development of the town.

In 1920, Chatterton declined to accept an appointment offered by Governor Robert D. Carey to be a judge in the judicial district of Fremont, Natrona and Converse Counties. In 1927, Governor Emerson offered him a position on the Public Service Commission and the State Board of Equalization. Chatterton agreed and moved to Cheyenne to fulfill his six-year term. He also resumed his law practice in Cheyenne, finally retiring in 1937. Thereafter, he moved to his last home northwest of Arvada, Colorado. In 1954, he was given an honorary doctorate of law degree by the University of Wyoming at the age of ninety-four. Fenimore Chatterton died on May 9, 1958, and was buried in Lakeview Cemetery.

# 14

# BLACK LEADERS

## *Founders of Church and Business*

**B**lack Americans played a variety of roles in the exploration and settlement of Cheyenne and Wyoming. The first Black settlers came to Wyoming early in the nineteenth century to work as scouts, hunters, trappers, traders and guides. Those who arrived in Cheyenne often worked as railroad workers, cowboys, business operators and founders of churches and other organizations.

### LUCINDA "LUCY" PHILLIPS

Lucy Phillips arrived in Cheyenne in 1867 at the age of sixty-two. She was born into slavery in Kentucky on April 22, 1804. She married Legrand Phillips while she was still enslaved. At the conclusion of the Civil War, she married Legrand for a second time so that the marriage would be legal following their freedom from slavery.

Lucy arrived by train in Cheyenne and quickly became known in the city. She was instrumental in establishing the city's first Black church, the African Methodist church at Eighteenth Street and Thomes

Reverend Katherine Fitzhugh portrayed Lucy Phillips at the Lakeview Cemetery Living History Walk in 2022. *Starley Talbott photograph.*

Avenue. The AME Church stood at that location for many years but was replaced by other buildings in later years. Lucy Phillips remained an active member of the church until her death in 1910 at the age of 106.

## HENRY JEFFERSON

Born into slavery in Missouri on August 15, 1856, Henry Jefferson left home at an early age. He went west by laying track for the railroad. He eventually arrived in Cheyenne, Wyoming, after he stopped working for the railroad.

He thrived in Cheyenne, where he opened his own business as a wallpaper hanger, and he developed a material for cleaning wallpaper.

Henry married Lula Jones in Missouri, and the couple returned to make their home in Cheyenne. They were among the charter members of the city's original African Methodist church. Henry was known for his vibrant voice, and he sang in the choir at church. Two daughters, Lillian and Pereta, were born to the Jeffersons. Pereta died at age twelve of scarlet fever. Lillian became an accomplished pianist and often accompanied her father.

Lula died in 1913. Henry married Hattie Ingram in 1919 and died on July 29, 1935.

## WILLIAM WITT

William Witt was stationed in Cuba and the Philippines with the United States Army before being assigned to Fort Francis E. Warren in Cheyenne. Witt was a veteran of the Spanish-American War, and he was a trumpeter in the military band.

William and his wife, Pearl, lived at Fort Warren for several years. They were the parents of four children, Willie, Marjorie, Dorothy and Christine, who attended Churchill Elementary School in Cheyenne.

After leaving the army, Witt became a brakeman with the Union Pacific Railroad in Cheyenne. Pearl established a laundry and catering business. They owned a home on West Seventeenth Street. The children attended junior and high school in Cheyenne, graduated from various colleges and were accomplished in various fields of endeavor. William died on February 23, 1960, and Pearl died on March 13, 1969.

# 15

# LAKEVIEW'S JAPANESE PLOT

## *Railroad Workers and Business Leaders*

In the southeast corner of Lakeview Cemetery, there are two areas known as the potter's field and the Japanese plot. There are approximately ninety people with Japanese surnames buried in these two areas.

Many of the people buried in this area came to Wyoming in the early 1900s as low-wage contract laborers for the Union Pacific Railroad. Many of the men died in railroad accidents. Because of the anti-Japanese sentiment that existed at the time, their deaths were seldom reported or were often trivialized in newspapers. If the person's estate did not have the five-dollar fee needed to give them a proper burial, they were buried in the potter's field.

A railroad section hand was struck by a train and treated for blood poisoning at St. John's Hospital but died six weeks later. A train accident west of Cheyenne in 1908 claimed the lives of nine men. The newspaper said the victims were "six railroad men and three Japanese victims." Another railroad worker died on February 11, 1912, from an injury received in the railyards. The newspaper headline read: "Jap Killed at U.P. Shops in Fly Wheel."

A section of the cemetery known as the Japanese plot was created in 1924. The headstones in this area display Japanese assimilation into western culture. Nestled among the markers etched with Japanese characters are headstones written in English or a combination of Japanese and English.

*Left*: Dan Lyon portrayed Japanese Joe, a representative of the typical Japanese railroad worker, at the Lakeview Cemetery Living History Walk in 2022. *Starley Talbott photograph.*

*Below*: The tombstone of Unosuke Ihata from Miwasaki Town, Higashimuro-gun, Wakayana Prefectore, Japan. He died on September 21, 1925, at the age of fifty-four and was buried in Lakeview Cemetery. Translation provided by Hisano Bell. *Starley Talbott photograph.*

Though little is known about many of the Japanese people who lived in Cheyenne in the early 1900s, some of their stories, especially those of the women, were recorded in a handwritten diary by Mrs. Frank Allyn. The diary was started in 1923 and recorded the activities of the women's ministry at the First Baptist Church. The group held an Americanization program to evangelize and teach American living skills to Cheyenne's Japanese community, who came to the city to work with the Union Pacific Railroad. Many of these Japanese men and women also operated businesses in Cheyenne.

## SELECTED DIARY ENTRIES

May 1923: "I was appointed chairman of the Christian Americanization for Cheyenne."

September 21: "The volunteers for Christian Americanization work met at my home to help plan the opening of the work with the Japanese women."

September 27: "Mrs. J. Harper, Mrs. Frank Emerson and Mrs. Ivan Rile went with me to the home of Mrs. Futa in the colony, where we opened the work with the women. Classes were opened in English and hand work with fifteen women enrolled."

December 27: "At Christmastime the Japanese women presented each of us (who opened up the Christian Americanization Work) a beautiful tea set."

January 15, 1924: "We moved our classes to the church, but the weather was too cold for the women to bring their children with them to class."

June 13: "I explained to the Missionary Society that owing to the Baptist State Conventions withdrawal of the Women's Work from the Rocky Mountain District, the Christian Americanization Work is left without a head. I suggested that the society take over the work and it was voted that they do so."

June 17: "The classes met at the recreation center. The Japanese women expressed their wish to learn American cooking. It was decided to meet at the church kitchen and demonstrate the making of lemon pie."

June 24: "After opening exercises, the class went to the kitchen. The teacher assisted the Japanese women to write out the recipe for lemon pie and give explanations where necessary. The pupils took the pies home and tried out the recipes during the week. One of the women reported that she made lemon pies for three days in succession. They asked to be taught how to make plain cake next time and they were to bring the materials."

July 8: "The classes were called together for a few minutes for special work, after which Mrs. Brady demonstrated the making of plain cake.

The women first copied the recipe, and then they assisted in measuring ingredients and gave strict attention to every detail. The cake when finished was very good."

July 22: "Giving to this being the week of Frontier Celebration, no classes were held."

July 29: "After the opening exercises, we discussed the subject of holding a picnic and decided to go to Pioneer Park on Saturday, August 1, at 10:30 for an outing this closing the year's work."

August 1: "The day was ideal for a picnic. Thirty-six adults and children met at Pioneer Park for the outing, planned by the teachers. We were sorry that on account of the mumps some of our Japanese friends were absent. Many games were played and there were plenty of good things to eat."

August 16: "The First Baptist Church was the scene of the wedding of T. Hashimoto and Hatsuye Murkawa. The teachers gave gift tokens of our best wishes for a long and happy wedded life."

September 9: "We reopened our classes with an enrollment of eleven women. It was decided to have sewing classes at the YWCA the second and fourth Wednesdays."

November 4: "Election day. Our meeting place on the south side being a voting place, our school met in the ladies' parlor of the church."

December 20: "All the Japanese children were invited to a Christmas party. Fruit cake was served with tea to the ladies, and the children were given popcorn balls and candy."

April 20, 1926: "Two new women arrived from Seattle and wish to study English. They are Mrs. Kono and Mrs. Matsushima. Mrs. Kono has a baby girl about 10 months old."

May 19: "After class was a demonstration of making strawberry shortcake and tuna fish salad. Lately we have made sandwiches and meat loaf. The sewing class had charge of the meeting on May 8 and gave a demonstration on work accomplished."

June 28: "Mrs. Kono took suddenly ill with brain fever and lived only three days. The teachers sent flowers and attended the funeral. We are sorry to lose such a fine woman from our number. It is sad too that the little girl is left motherless."

July 12: "I have been asked to take care of the baby. She is a good little thing, and I am sure I shall have no trouble. She will be 1 year old on the 23rd. Her name is Kimuye. Her father works in the railroad shops. Her mother was a barber and worked in the shop with Mr. and Mrs. Matsushima."

The burial of Mrs. Kono at Lakeview Cemetery. Mr. Kono, holding his baby, can be seen on the left with Mr. and Mrs. Matsushima on either side of him. *Wyoming State Archives, Department of State Parks and Cultural Resources.*

A memorial for Kiku Matsushima, a barber in Cheyenne who died on February 27, 1927, shortly after giving birth. *Starley Talbott photograph.*

A photograph of Mr. Kono and his daughter Kimuye. *Wyoming State Archives, Department of State Parks and Cultural Resources.*

September 29: "English classes were re-opened, and various activities continued through December, 1926."

February 27, 1927: "We were shocked to hear of the sudden death of Mrs. Matshushima. She gave birth to a baby girl and died two hours after. The teachers sent flowers and attended the funeral. Mr. Matsushima found an American home for his baby."

January 31, 1928: "A birthday party was given at the church in the honor of babies born since we opened our C.A. work. The two motherless babies were showered with gifts, and a gift and birthday cake was given to each of the others. We were glad that we gave the party, as Mr. Kono came on February 6 to take the baby to Utah with him. She had been in our home one year and seven months. We became very much attached to her and missed her very much. He expects to take her to Japan in July."

May 30, 1935: Mrs. Allyn summarized the work of the organization with these words:

> As Japanese children became of school age, a few parents enrolled them in the public school, but most of them took them back to Japan to be educated. By 1935, several families of our work had returned to Japan, which included about 15 women and 30 children.
>
> About 1935, the Union Pacific System extended their Cheyenne shop yards south, which necessitated the moving of the row of houses where the Japanese lived. The Japanese families who remained in Cheyenne and those who came later located in various locations in residential sections. A few children and women still attend Sunday school and other services. We correspond with several women who returned to Japan who tell us of their continued living of the Christian life and letting their light shine. Some are doing real missionary work in their village churches. Our church women keep in contact with Japanese homes by calling and ministering in various ways. Most of the women and children we had in our early Christian Americanization work returned to Japan before 1941.

## OTHER JAPANESE EMPLOYMENT IN CHEYENNE

Many Japanese operated business enterprises, ranging from art stores and grocery stores to restaurants and barbershops. There was a vibrant Japanese business community on West Seventeenth Street for many years. Those buildings no longer exist.

# 16

# JOSEPH MAULL CAREY

## *Grand Old Man*

There are few figures in Wyoming's history who have contributed so much to the success of the territory and the then young state as Joseph Maull Carey. First arriving as a federal official to take care of the new Wyoming Territory, Carey eventually became the state's governor and one of its most respected citizens.

Joseph Maul Carey was born on January 19, 1845, in Milton, Delaware. He was the third of seven children born to Robert Hood, a wealthy manufacturer, and Susan Davis Carey. Joseph's education began in local private and public schools. He proved to be an excellent student and even taught in a small country school near his home for a time. Joseph entered the Fort Edward Collegiate Institute in Fort Edward, New York, which was widely known at the time for its college preparatory courses. He later attended Union College in Schenectady, New York, which he attended through his sophomore year.

In 1865, at the age of twenty, Joseph moved to Philadelphia to study law in the office of B.F. Temple and then in the office of W.L. Dennis and Henry Flanders. While working for these law firms, he also attended the University of Pennsylvania Law School and graduated in 1867. During his last years as a law student, Joseph began to take a significant interest in politics, stumping in both Pennsylvania in 1866 in support of the reelection of Governor Geary and then in 1868 in New Jersey campaigns to boost the Republican Party in its campaign to elect Ulysses S. Grant to the presidency.

Carey's youthful enthusiasm and the excellent credentials he earned as a student brought him to the attention of Grant, who appointed the twenty-three-year-old as the first territorial attorney general for Wyoming Territory. Carey was twenty-four years old when he stepped off the train onto Wyoming soil for the first time. He immediately impressed people, particularly Governor Joseph Campbell, with his excellent speaking abilities and formidable legal acumen. In his profession, Carey took part in setting up all the legal details of governing the young territory and tried all of the government's cases in the first year of Wyoming's existence. As new counties were being established, several hired Carey to manage their legal affairs until they could elect their own attorneys. His legal reputation became so formidable that in 1871, President Grant appointed him to the Wyoming Territorial Supreme Court at the age of twenty-six.

By this time, the cattle business was exploding across the territory's grasslands. Carey was sure that the new industry was the best way to make a fortune in the territory, and with the help of his brothers R. Davis Carey of Philadelphia and later Dr. John F. Carey, he quickly established his own ranching operation by 1871, when they purchased their first herd of five hundred cattle. He purchased land in the vicinity of the old Platte River Station on the Oregon Trail and built a log cabin on his property with his own hands. This humble beginning grew to become the mighty CY Ranch, the oldest registered brand in the territory, near present-day Casper, Wyoming. By 1876, the ranch contained fifteen thousand head of cattle, and Carey had attained considerable wealth.

Carey's strident interest and support of the cattle industry led him to become deeply involved with the new Wyoming Stock Growers Association after it was established in 1873. He was present at all of the association's early meetings and became president from 1883 to 1887. To foster the association's growth and influence, Carey frequently made trips east to garner investment in the WSGA. His work helped build the association into the most successful organization of its kind in the world, with membership investments totaling $200 million and considerable sway in Wyoming, Colorado, the Dakota Territory, Idaho, Montana, Nebraska and Utah. Ranching was central to Carey's financial well-being, but his interests continued to pull him in other directions.

In 1872, Carey's attention was drawn outside Wyoming when he became part of the United States Centennial Commission, a function he would continue to serve in through 1876. Continuing with his ardent participation in politics, he served as the Wyoming's representative to the

Joseph M. Carey was a delegate to Congress for Wyoming Territory and the first U.S. senator from Wyoming from 1890 to 1895. He was the eighth governor of Wyoming from 1911 to 1915. *Wyoming State Archives, Department of State Parks and Cultural Resources.*

Republican National Committee from 1876 to 1897. In 1876, he was named commissioner of Wyoming Territory for the 1876 World's Fair in Philadelphia. The year of the national centennial also saw Carey attain the height of Wyoming society. By that time, he had grown so wealthy that he was able to build the largest and most lavishly appointed house in the Cheyenne. Eventually, the people of the City of Cheyenne renamed Ferguson Street Carey Avenue, which still bears his name.

Joseph pursued more intimate and personal matters when he married Louisa Davis in 1877. Louisa had recently moved to Wyoming with her family from Dubuque, Iowa, when her father, Edward C. Davis, became the territorial surveyor. Joseph and Louisa would have two sons, Robert D. and Charles D. Carey.

Carey re-entered politics in Cheyenne in 1880. Having a strong desire to see his adopted hometown succeed, Carey ran and was elected mayor of Cheyenne on the platform of bringing a stable water and sewage system to the capital city. The project was undertaken in 1882 and 1883 and provided the city four hundred thousand gallons of water daily, enough to meet the needs of fifty thousand people. Similarly, Carey pushed to install a suitable sewer system commensurate with the community's needs. Both systems were constructed for $150,000.

While the water infrastructure was being built, Carey also oversaw the substantial development of the downtown business district, with many of the buildings that were constructed still intact today. Many citizens, by 1884, attributed the growth and attractive appearance of the city's businesses and homes to Carey's considerable efforts. He was also credited with the planting of trees in the city, establishing the first electric streetlights and the hiring of a Black police officer. Carey also established an ordinance banning livestock from wandering the city's streets and established that all sidewalks in the city were to be made of concrete or another solid substance.

Another important achievement was implemented by Carey when Congress began debating the closure of Fort D.A. Russell in the early 1880s. Carey traveled to confer with officials in Chicago and Washington about the matter. He not only saved the fort from being closed but also secured more than $100,000 for its enlargement.

With large amounts of wealth, Carey became deeply involved in several other business ventures, which led him to have a close association with Francis E. Warren. The first of these joint ventures was the establishment of the Brush-Swan Electric Company in Cheyenne in 1882. The company was contracted with the city to run electricity to twenty-two streetlamps. This venture became one of the first electric companies in the nation, and it later combined with Warren's Cheyenne Gas Company and became the Cheyenne Light, Fuel and Power Company. Carey later became a trustee for the Cheyenne and Northern Railroad, again in conjunction with Warren.

In November 1884, Carey was selected by the Wyoming territorial legislature to be its representative to the U.S. Congress, a position he would hold for the next six years. In 1885, when Chester A. Arthur was looking for a resident citizen to become the governor of Wyoming Territory, Carey prevailed upon Congress and the president to select Francis E. Warren.

In the spring of 1890, Carey presented the bill to the United States House of Representatives to admit Wyoming as the forty-fourth state. Despite accusations that the state didn't have the suitable population to be considered for statehood and that granting statehood to a territory that had allowed women the right to vote would be a mistake, Carey's arguments prevailed. Wyoming became a state on July 10, 1890. In gratitude and recognition of his considerable contribution, Carey was named Wyoming's first United States senator, and Francis E. Warren was nominated as the second.

The two men did not have a smooth political relationship in Washington, D.C., and this relationship grew worse over the "Free Silver" issue that dominated Congress in the 1892 session. Carey came down on the side of supporting gold as the basis of the dollar with the rest of the Republican Party. Warren came down on the side of silver, supporting the will of his constituents in Wyoming.

In Wyoming, Carey and Warren were perceived as having different levels of involvement with the conflict between cattle barons and small ranchers known as the Johnson County War. Warren was successful in conveying that he was caught by surprise by the invasion of Johnson County. Carey, on the other hand, was widely perceived to have been one of the principal players in the organization of the invasion. While Carey's direct involvement was never proved, the political winds shifted against him. Perceiving this shift in Wyoming politics, Carey declined to run for re-election to the United States Congress in 1895.

Prior to his departure from congress, Carey sponsored one of the most significant land acts in the history of the American West. The Carey Land Act granted one million acres of arid federal lands to all states in the West. The land, which was located within a state's borders, was to be under the control of the new states but irrigated at their own expense. The project proved vastly successful in Wyoming and throughout the West. In Wyoming, it aided in the settlement of the Big Horn Basin and many other locations throughout the state.

The Carey Land Act, approved in 1894, allowed anyone over the age of twenty-one to claim 640 acres of land and apply water to the land to obtain a patent. The Wyoming Development Company was formed in the Wheatland area to oversee the project in southern Wyoming. In 1883, work had been started on an irrigation project that would transfer water from the Laramie River through a series of canals to be delivered to the Wheatland area. The development company drilled a tunnel through solid rock in the Laramie Mountains to carry water from the Laramie River to the newly created Wheatland Colony. The project was completed in 1886. The company had control of the land through the allocation of water rights, and settlers, under the Carey Land Act, took up the acreages. After a farmer received a patent and full payment was made for the water right, a deed was issued. The Wyoming Development Company eventually became the Wheatland Irrigation District, a private company that still operates.

Joseph M. Carey (*center*) in front of the Wyoming State Capitol with dogs, horses and men in uniform around 1910. *Wyoming State Archives, Department of State Parks and Cultural Resources.*

In 1905, along with John H. Gordon and Elwood Mead, Carey founded the Wyoming State Fair. It was first held in Cheyenne and then in Casper for its second year. From 1907 onward, the fair was held in Douglas.

In 1910, Carey attempted to run for governor on the Republican ticket but failed to secure the party's nomination. He then switched parties and was successfully elected. During his term as governor, Carey worked tirelessly to dismantle political machines by opening election primaries to the public. He also helped pass the Corrupt Practice Act, making it harder for anyone who attempted to buy elections.

In 1912, Carey and six other prominent politicians helped found Teddy Roosevelt's Progressive Party. When the opportunity arose for him to be reelected to the governorship, Carey declined. In his mind, he did not want to be his own successor but instead believed that a governor should get four years to make their impact on the state and then pass the responsibility on to another. Of his term, he was pleased with the ongoing reclamation of land for irrigation, the efforts of protecting the livestock industry from harmful diseases and the state geologist's office working hard on developing the state's mineral wealth. Labor and industry seemed to get along and manage their differences well, and taxes were not a heavy burden.

Upon the expiration of his term as governor, Carey stepped down and quietly went back into private life. During the next several years, Carey appeared in public on multiple occasions, lauding the promise of Wyoming and speaking about the early history of the state and its rugged pioneers and letting his political opinion be known on the state and national level. He stayed out of the limelight after his son was elected governor in November 1918, and on February 6, 1924, Joseph M. Carey passed away quietly in his home after a long illness.

Following the death of the elder statesman of Wyoming, tributes poured in from Wyoming's governor William B. Ross and several other dignitaries who had worked alongside Carey through the years. His service to the City of Cheyenne and the State of Wyoming were difficult to sum up. For more than fifty years, he worked for the benefit of the state and its citizens. There have been few other politicians or citizens who have left such an enduring and indelible mark on Wyoming and its history.

# 17

# ROBERT D. CAREY

## *A Broken Friendship Is Healed*

When Robert D. Carey was born in Cheyenne on August 12, 1878, he couldn't have arrived under more auspicious circumstances. His father was Joseph Maull Carey, one of the most upstanding and wealthy men of Wyoming Territory. His father, despite being deeply involved in the Wyoming Stock Growers Association and running the oldest ranch in the territory, was attentive to his young son. Doted on by his mother, Louisa, in their magnificent home, Robert was born with a silver spoon in both hands.

While growing up in the capital city, Robert attended Cheyenne's public schools. His father was eager for him to join him in the ranching business, and he accompanied his father frequently to their CY Ranch at the foot of Casper Mountain. He remembered making his first trip there on a buckboard wagon at the age of four. He remembered staying in the abandoned cabins at Fort Caspar while his father brought down logs from the mountain to make their cabin on the ranch.

The Careys were eager to make sure that Robert had the best education possible and sent him to Hill School in Pottstown, Pennsylvania, and later Yale. He achieved a bachelor's degree at Yale and returned to Wyoming to help his father's growing enterprises. Working for his father's firm, J.M. Carey and Brother, Robert excelled.

Shortly after Robert's return from Yale, his father appointed him manager for the central Wyoming section of the family's ranching operations in Laramie, Converse and Natrona Counties. One of the family's holdings was the old S.O. Ranch in Converse County that had once belonged to Wyoming pioneer John Hunton. Robert assumed the management of this operation and began a series of experiments that would have long-term dividends. In addition to running the usual cattle, he devoted hundreds of the ranch's acres to sugar beets, alfalfa and small grains, all using an irrigation system of his own design. His system of crop raising proved so successful that he had to build a private rail system to handle the four thousand tons of sugar beets he produced annually. Robert also entered his produce at national fairs and won multiple awards at competitions in Sacramento and St. Louis. He also joined his father in the Wyoming Development Company, Wyoming's first large-scale irrigation project on the Wheatland flats north of Cheyenne.

Along with his business success, Robert met and married Julia B. Freeman, the daughter of Brigadier General H.B. Freeman, a general during the Philippine Insurrection. After a whirlwind courtship, they were married in Douglas in 1903. The couple eventually became the parents of a daughter and a son.

Robert followed his father's involvement in the Wyoming Stock Growers Association by serving as vice-president from 1908 to 1910 and again from 1912 to 1913. He eventually became president of the Wyoming Stock Growers Association from 1915 to 1919.

In 1912, Joseph Maull Carey was elected governor of Wyoming, and Robert served as his secretary. Like his father, Robert was a staunch Republican. Also like his father, he was willing to buck the party to support Teddy Roosevelt's newly formed Progressive Party and was a delegate for Wyoming in 1912. Eventually, both men returned to the Republican fold, and in 1918, Robert decided to run for governor. During this contest, Joseph's bitter political rival and onetime friend Francis E. Warren threw his support behind Robert. This magnanimous gesture and the warm support from Warren for his son healed the breach between the Joseph Carey and Francis Warren. Robert was also buoyed by the outspoken support for his candidacy from Teddy Roosevelt, who wrote:

> *I regard you as among the ablest and most farsighted public servants in the country; and you possess in marked degree the saving grace of common sense. I feel that your election would mean very much for Wyoming and for our whole country; and as a good American citizen, I earnestly wish success to you and to Senator Warren* [who was also seeking reelection], *and to all your other associates on the ticket.*

On November 5, 1918, Robert Carey became governor elect for the State of Wyoming. The nation was in the waning days of World War I but was facing a tremendous battle with the newly arrived Spanish influenza, which was devastating the country and driving society to unprecedented levels of emergency and fear. Due to the strict quarantine put in place in Cheyenne to combat the Spanish influenza, Robert took the oath of office in a quiet ceremony on January 5, 1919. Taking the oath of office on the same Bible that his father had used, newspapers were quick to note that Robert Carey was the first native son of Wyoming to become its governor. All previous governors had been born elsewhere.

At the same time, the nation was faced with the choice of being a wet or a dry country. Many Wyoming newspapers were clamoring for the state to renounce liquor in all its forms. One of Governor Carey's first official duties was to oversee the Wyoming legislature in its ratification of the national prohibition amendment. It was the first bill to go before the legislature in

Robert Carey (third from the left) served as the Wyoming governor from 1919 to 1923. Others in this photograph include U.S. senator F.E. Warren, Governor Nellie Tayloe Ross and Senator John Kendrick, circa 1925. *Wyoming State Archives, Department of State Parks and Cultural Resources.*

1919 and the first that Carey signed into law. The measure became effective on July 1, a full year before national prohibition was to be activated, and enforcement of the law proved to be very difficult throughout Carey's administration. The state was soon beset by bootleggers and common citizens willing to buck the law.

The rest of Robert Carey's political career as governor was relatively smooth. Historian T.A. Larson noticed that he got most of what he asked the legislature for, which itself was noted as being particularly nonpartisan and efficient. Carey's major achievements included the passage of the Blue-Sky Law, granting significant compensation increases for state officers, funding for the expansion of the state's highway system and improvements for state institutions and greater support for workmen's compensation.

Robert was also instrumental in reactivating the state's Immigration Commission, which had been unfunded for years. With the end of World War I, Robert saw great potential for the open spaces of Wyoming to draw in vast numbers of new immigrants who were looking at taking advantage of the new lands the state had opened to reclamation. Unfortunately, the summer of 1919 saw the onset of a long, bitter drought that would eventually lead to the ruin of many of these new farmers and bring the effects of an economic depression to the state far earlier than they arrived in the rest of the United States. On his watch, the state also weathered a series of national strikes on the railroads and coal mines that depressed the economy of the state further. On the positive side, it was widely perceived that his financial management of the state was entirely sound and even beneficial to the Wyoming taxpayer, as many of his policies cleaned up the operations of many state administrations and even increased the funding of high schools around Wyoming boosting their attendance during his term by 300 percent.

On a livelier note, in July 1919, Robert was emerging from the Wyoming State Capitol when he was startled by a horse ridden by Mrs. Jack Elliot, a renowned cowgirl, which had charged down Capitol Avenue and up the steps straight to him. The woman handed him a letter from women who were concerned that Cheyenne Frontier Days™ was going to use a non-Wyoming resident as part of its new "Miss Wyoming" campaign to boost the event. This campaign, the brainchild of the Union Pacific Railroad, was the first coordinated national effort to bring more visitors to the western celebration. The main focus of the effort was to name the first queen of the rodeo, who would travel the nation, visiting dignitaries and delivering invitations. These invitations, it turned out, were to come from Carey's own hand and were addressed to President Wilson, Senator

Warren G. Harding and the mayors of Omaha, Chicago, New York, Philadelphia, Pittsburgh, Kansas City and several other cities. Carey was a good sport throughout the whole affair and wished Helen Bonham, the young woman chosen for the task, complete success. He and Helen worked together for the next three years, trying to get the president of the United States and others to come to Wyoming.

Another interesting occurrence happened in August, when Lieutenant Colonel Dwight Eisenhower arrived in Hillsdale on an army expedition. His goal was to ascertain the viability of transporting troops and trucks across the United States. Carey was on hand to greet Eisenhower. The troops were then given a special Wild West celebration at Frontier Park and were allowed to rest and recuperate at Fort D.A. Russell

In 1920, the issue of granting women the right to vote came across Carey's desk. The Nineteenth Amendment was hotly contested across the country, and Therese Jenkins, Wyoming's strongest advocate for women's suffrage, called on Carey to ensure his support for the amendment with a special session of the Wyoming legislature. Carey readily agreed and arranged for the session to run from January 26 to 28. To the assembled delegates, he issued the following statement:

> *Recently it has become apparent, to obtain the requisite number of states that action on the part of this state may be absolutely necessary. Further, the opponents of suffrage have been using as an argument against granting equal rights to women that Wyoming had not ratified for the reason that suffrage had proved a failure in this state. We could not allow such a charge to be unchallenged.*

The Wyoming Senate ratified the amendment unanimously on January 26, and the house followed suit on January 28. Wyoming's position as the territory that had granted women the right to the vote in 1869, which was upheld at its granting of statehood in 1890, would not be questioned.

Despite Robert Carey's remarkable record while in office, circumstances that were beyond his control forced him from office. By August 1922, the economic and political climate turned volatile. The struggling people of the state didn't think Carey did enough to alleviate their growing sorrows, and he was rejected by his own party during the primaries in August that year.

With the death of Joseph Carey in 1924, the considerable holdings of the Carey family passed into Robert's hands, which he managed from the S.O.

Ranch near Casper. He also continued the family's support for the City of Casper. For years, the family had donated land to the new community, having formerly established the town with the arrival of the Fremont, Elkhorn and Missouri Valley Railroad in the area. Their continued support went to the donation of land for churches, municipal buildings, the Carnegie Library, entire city blocks and even a city park.

Robert's national involvement in politics also grew during this time. In 1924, President Calvin Coolidge appointed him chairman of a commission that was established to investigate the agricultural situation of the United States at the time. Of his work on the commission following Carey's submission of its findings, Coolidge wrote a letter to him, stating, "I feel that you have performed a very valuable public service, which has done more, perhaps, than anything else could have done to clarify the public mind in relation to farm problems."

Wyoming was shaken by the death of its preeminent citizen Francis E. Warren in Washington, D.C., on November 24, 1929. Robert Carey announced his candidacy to finish the unexpired term of Senator Warren in the upcoming election. He won the election and took the oath of office on December 1, 1930, forty years to the day after his father did in 1890 as Wyoming's first senator.

As Wyoming's senator, Carey completed Warren's remaining term and served another six years in the United States Senate. During his tenure, he was an ardent supporter of tariffs to protect livestock and industrial development in the West. He also continued to push for the federal government to release more lands to the control of Wyoming and for enduring support of irrigation and reclamation projects. He was wary of Franklin D. Roosevelt's New Deal programs, particularly the Agricultural Adjustment Administration, which was trying to implement a program of slaughtering hogs wholesale to drive up prices through artificial scarcity. However, he was in support of other New Deal initiatives, such as the Federal Deposit Insurance Law and the Social Security Act. Despite his consistent support for the initiatives he thought would benefit Wyoming, voters narrowly decided to back Carey's Democratic opponent and supporter of the New Deal programs Harry H. Schwartz in 1936.

Robert Carey returned to Wyoming, where he resumed his business interests. Unfortunately, he died of a heart attack in Cheyenne on January 17, 1937, at the age of fifty-eight. He was buried in the Carey family plot at Lakeview Cemetery.

# 18

# WILLIAM BRADFORD ROSS

## *Lawyer with a Zest for Politics*

When a handsome young lawyer and his bride arrived in Wyoming in 1902, they did not know their lives would have an impact on the history of the state. William and Nellie Ross began their married life in Cheyenne, where William had begun the practice of law one year earlier.

William Bradford Ross was born on December 4, 1873, to Ambrose B. Ross and Susan Grey. Ambrose, a resident of Dover, Tennessee, was the county clerk of Stewart County. Little is known about William's years growing up, but what is known is that he had a desire to enter the practice of law at an early age. For a time, he studied law at the offices of Chancellor J.W. Stout of the Sixth Tennessee Division and graduated from Peabody College in Nashville around 1900.

After graduating, Ross practiced law in Tennessee for three years before heading west and establishing his first law practice in Cheyenne in 1901. He met Nellie Tayloe at a family gathering in Tennessee, and the two were married in Omaha on September 14, 1902. She remembered him as "an ardent young southerner, a lawyer with zest for politics in his blood, and sharing his interest, my own quickened and deepened with every passing year."

In 1904, Ross took up the fight against gambling in Cheyenne when he filed a brief to the Wyoming Supreme Court in support of the 1901 State Anti-Gambling legislation. The bill had been passed by the legislature, but Speaker Tidball did not sign the bill prior to the legislature's adjournment. From that time, opponents of the bill argued that Tidball's failure to sign the bill negated the law's legitimacy. Gambling operators were pleased to continue to operate in the ambiguity of the situation, and the Wyoming legislature had never corrected the issue.

Cheyenne businessman Harry P. Hynds asked the Laramie County commissioners to grant him a license to open a gambling establishment, and they refused to do so. The case was elevated to the Wyoming Supreme Court for determination. Laramie County prosecuting attorney Walter R. Stoll decided to step away from the case, and friends of the measure retained Ross to take his place. Ross argued that the legislature's intent to pass the law was sufficient, as was the governor's signature, regardless of whether the speaker signed the bill. His argument would, in turn, validate a number of Wyoming laws that had suffered the same fate, many of which regarded provisions for the punishment for crimes. Ultimately, the supreme court sided with Ross's position, and he was given credit for saving Wyoming's antigambling laws. He and others were frustrated, however, that few local officials were willing to make efforts to enforce the law.

In 1904, Ross formally entered politics when he ran to become the Laramie County prosecuting attorney as a Democrat against the Republican incumbent Walter R. Stoll. The election was exceptionally close, and the final tabulation of the votes determined that Ross had won by only twenty votes. Stoll refused to concede and continued to occupy the office of the Laramie County prosecuting attorney. The courts could not make an immediate determination of the election's outcome and determined that Ross could assume the duties of the prosecuting attorney until such time as the matter could be sorted out. Ross was sworn into office by County Clerk T. Joe Cahill on January 6, 1905. The courts were finally able to begin hearing arguments in the case of *Stoll v. Ross* exactly four months later, and the final ruling was made on September 6. During the course of arguments, it was revealed that there was evidence that ballots were doctored by an unknown person in two precincts. However, the court declared Ross the winner.

With the messy business of the election behind him, Ross began to pursue his chief objective with relish. He was determined to enforce Wyoming's 1901 antigambling law and filed suits against many businessmen who were running slot machines in their establishments. Complaints against six men, including Harry Hynds and his Capitol Resort, were filed, and the fines were significant. Each breach of the law entailed a fine between $300 and $1,000 and a jail term lasting three months to a year. The shock of this move forced the city's known gambling establishments to close their doors the next day, making the occasion the first time the capital city was without operating

William Ross, the governor of Wyoming from January 1, 1923, to October 2, 1924. *Wyoming State Archives, Department of State Parks and Cultural Resources.*

gambling establishments in its history. For the rest of his term, Ross fought against not only gambling but also the sale of alcohol and prize fighting.

In 1908, Ross won a seat in the Wyoming Senate. Two years later, at the age of thirty-seven, Ross campaigned for a seat in the United States Congress against Republican incumbent Frank Mondell. Ross was firm in his belief that it was high time for the government to be taken out of the hands of special interests and to be returned to the people. Ross lost his bid and returned to his law practice.

In 1922, Ross emerged again as the favored Democratic candidate, this time for Wyoming's governorship. Wyoming had fallen into a deep depression, and the people of the state were suffering relentless economic blows. The main thrust of his platform was to make sure that the rent and royalties of Wyoming mineral wealth should be used to reduce the tax burdens on the average citizen. There were opponents of this point of view who believed that it would be better to cut the state's expenses instead.

Even within the Democratic Party, members thought the policies of Ross were too radical and sought to supplant him. Nonetheless, Ross garnered enough support to face Republican John Hay. Realizing that he had to convince his own party of his worthiness, Ross canvased the state, rigorously giving numerous addresses in every county of the state. This proved very beneficial, as many Wyomingites appreciated his speaking ability and persuasive demeanor. He also appealed to citizens who were concerned with the effects of illegal alcohol on the state, promising to uphold the prohibition laws. It proved to be a bitter, divisive campaign. Ross won the governorship by a margin of 638 votes.

Ross pledged to the citizens of the state that he would work to bring a higher standard of living to the state's residents, reduce expenses, lower taxes, foment a greater regard for law and strive for a higher level of citizenship. He planned to abolish all useless offices, consolidate departments as much as possible and work for economy and efficiency.

Governor Ross also pledged to reform the collection of taxes. He called out the large corporate interests who were not residents of the state and who paid taxes only on the output of their efforts, not the property they held within the state's borders. He stated they were taking wealth out of the state, only to generate more wealth and add jobs and revenue for other states. Ross also pledged to uphold the prohibition laws, believing that the ills of alcohol and the dangers of illegal production far outweighed their benefits. He knew that enforcement was unpopular, but the law was to be upheld as well as all others justly employed by the state.

Ross continued to implement his vision of how to help the state weather its difficult circumstances. His most significant achievement of his early administration was the submission of a constitutional amendment officially allowing for severance taxes to be placed on Wyoming's mineral wealth.

In the fall of 1924, Ross was attending a forum in Laramie in support of the severance tax. Several people near him noticed that he wasn't as full of enthusiasm and vigor as usual. He underwent emergency surgery the next day for acute appendicitis. His appendix was removed, but Ross developed septic phlebitis and died at 3:15 a.m. on October 2, 1924, at the age of fifty-one.

Upon his death, Frank E. Lucas, the secretary of state, assumed the governorship until a special election could be held. Ross left behind three sons and his bereaved wife, Nellie. Fate soon intervened to bring about a historic moment for the state of Wyoming.

# 19

# NELLIE TAYLOE ROSS

## *First in the Nation*

When Nellie saw her home in Cheyenne, Wyoming, for the first time, she anticipated that she would probably spend the rest of her life there. A resident of Missouri, Nellie had met and married William Bradford Ross after a brief engagement. She loved and admired the young attorney who had set up his first law practice in the city only a year prior to their marriage. She anticipated that she would be a good wife to him, endeavoring to take care of the home and family they hoped to start. Nellie had no idea at the time that her home would house not one but two future governors.

Nellie Tayloe was born on November 29, 1876, near St. Joseph, Missouri. Her mother, Lizzie Green, had come from a wealthy slave-owning family in northwestern Missouri who was left destitute after the Civil War. Her father, James Tayloe, married Lizzie, inherited the Green farm and attempted to manage it for a time. When this proved impossible, he sold the farm after Nellie was born and moved the family to Miltonvale, Kansas, in 1884, where he became a grocer. Nellie was prone to frequent illnesses as a child. She attended school when she could, and the family hired private tutors to maintain her education. In 1892, Nellie finished her schooling and moved with her family to Omaha after their fortunes collapsed. There, she completed coursework that allowed her to teach kindergarten. She obtained her first job as a teacher in Omaha, Nebraska, yet she was only able to stay in that position until her health failed after two years. In 1900, she met William Bradford Ross at a gathering of the Tayloe family in Paris, Tennessee. The two wrote letters to each other afterward and fell in love. In 1902, Nellie and William were married in Omaha and moved to Cheyenne.

While William was engaged in growing his law practice and, later, his political career, Nellie endeavored to stay in the background, taking care of their twin boys, George and Ambrose, who had been born in 1903. As a new arrival in the community, Nellie engaged in Cheyenne society and, like her friends and neighbors, took advantage of the unique ability of Wyoming women to vote. For most of her married life, that was the extent of her politics. Having a keen mind, however, she also took a deep interest in her husband's cases and political career. They had constant conversations about what was happening in his professional life. William tried out his legal theories on her, and through their frank and honest conversations, she began to absorb an understanding of the law and government that would prove to be invaluable.

The young couple struggled in the early years of their marriage, as neither came from a wealthy background, and they were struggling with the debts from William's legal education. The social life of the capital city was something they both enjoyed, but they entertained heavily, which strained their finances. The twins were often ill, and the tragedy of the death of their third son, Alfred, who was born in 1905, rocked the family.

Nellie felt that these early tribulations transformed her from a weak, young girl into a strong, self-reliant woman. The strong love within the family allowed them to persevere together. They were blessed with a fourth son, William Bradford Ross II, in 1912.

The growing family, with the prosperity granted by William's law practice, moved from their small bungalow into a large colonial-style home that still stands on Seventeenth Street in Cheyenne.

As her children grew older, Nellie was able to pursue more activities outside the home. One of her favorite activities was participating in the Cheyenne Woman's Club, which comprised twenty-five ladies. She had been invited to join the exclusive club, and she felt it was her duty to improve herself, despite the rigors of her domestic demands. The clubwomen often spoke before the membership on issues of politics, history, science or any topic that led to self-improvement of the speaker and listeners. In addition to the speeches, exhaustive papers had to be presented on the topics, and each woman could expect to speak two to three times a year. It was in this group that Nellie developed strong speaking and writing skills that proved helpful in the future.

Nellie was deeply involved in William's political preparations and problems. She did not, however, enjoy the campaigns and found them wearisome, as she made the following statement:

*In those days, not only did I not anticipate a political career for myself, I did not aspire to political honors for my husband. This was due partly to my ambition for him to shine in his profession. I confess, too, that I found the acrimonious controversies of political campaigns wearing, especially when they took my husband from home on long speaking trips, as they usually did—and they came so woefully often. It would not have been so distasteful to me if our part had more frequently been crowned with success. But Democrats were so distressingly in the minority in Wyoming that running for office on that ticket was simply to immolate oneself for the good of the party. My husband took his turn with the others. The love of politics was in his blood, and he was always in the thick of the fight. He believed in the principles of his party and, popular or not, fearlessly contended for them in and out of season.*

Through the ebbs and flows of her husband's political success, Nellie learned more about the operations of politics vicariously through William's efforts. After William failed to unseat Frank Mondell from the U.S. Senate in 1910, she prevailed upon him to forego running for political office again.

William acceded to her wishes and focused on his practice. In 1922, pressure from friends and allies for William to run for governor reached a fever pitch. With each letter and request, Nellie sought reassurance that he would not yield to the temptation, which he readily gave her. On the last day of filing, she suddenly had a change of heart and said, "Who am I to attempt to thwart a career that might prove to this husband of mine an everlasting satisfaction?"

With Nellie's blessing, William agreed to campaign and was elected governor of the state in 1922. The partnership between William and Nellie continued and profoundly affected their lives. The couple entered the executive mansion, located only a few blocks from their home, as deeply committed to their partnership as they ever had been. They worked tirelessly together, not only on the new trappings that would make the mansion their home, but also on the documents he was preparing for his inauguration and beyond.

Nellie found her experience as Wyoming's first lady to be wonderful, and she thoroughly enjoyed her role and responsibilities. Social duties that expanded her acquaintances and contacts throughout the state frequently occupied her time, but Nellie and William continued their conversations about his daily challenges and successes as they had done throughout his legal career. Occasionally, she would even finish preparing his speeches after he had to retire for the night.

The sudden death of her husband on October 2, 1924, due to complications from appendicitis, was a terrible shock for Nellie and the state of Wyoming. In the aftermath of her husband's death, she showed no emotion in public but was devastated in private. On the afternoon that her husband was buried, she was approached by close friends to see if she would run to fill the remainder of her husband's term.

Nellie's friends knew of the close partnership between the couple and were well aware of her role in forming Governor Ross's policies and positions. Nellie, mired in grief, hesitated. By the deadline of October 14, friends such as Tracy McCracken, Joseph C. O'Mahoney and others prevailed upon Nellie that she could do the job—and should. She accepted the challenge and filed to run forty-five minutes prior to the close of the registration period.

Against her Republican opponent, Eugene J. Sullivan of Casper, Nellie ran a unique campaign. Upon accepting the Democratic nomination, Nellie vowed to remain at home to grieve and to care for her family. The actual campaign was left to her friends. Very few speeches were offered on her behalf, and a few were offered by Wyoming's junior senator John B. Kendrick. Instead, the campaign was conducted through the posting of handbills and posters. Through them, Nellie proclaimed she would continue William B. Ross's policies.

Nellie won the governorship by eight thousand votes. In doing so, she became the first woman governor in the United States. She had narrowly won the honor, because Miriam "Ma" Ferguson was elected governor of Texas on the same date, but she was not inaugurated until fifteen days later. While many women suffragists hailed Nellie's election as a victory, others disagreed. Upon hearing that Miriam Ferguson was also successful in her bid for governor, one paper quipped that neither woman had "executed anything more constructive probably than baking a pie or making a bed."

The *New York Times* wondered if Nellie Ross would be addressed as "Governess? Governorine? Governette?" The paper settled on governor and wrote, "Why not? If they make good governors, it will not be because they are women, but because they have sense, intelligence and character, and if they make bad one—but of course they will not, and to give any thought to that abhorrent contingency would be discourteously premature and worthy only of a woman-hater."

For Nellie's part, she had her own ideas on the matter:

*Not for one moment did I doubt…whether I felt within myself the ability to fill the position. After I went into office, I realized more and more how much knowledge I had unconsciously absorbed of the affairs of the various departments responsible to the executive.*

As governor, Nellie was indeed up to the task and rapidly moved to continue her late husband's policies. She was so dedicated to her husband's vision for Wyoming that she retained the men he had chosen to help him run the government instead of installing her own. This was a severe disappointment to many women suffragists who had hoped Nellie would place more women in positions of government. Nellie thought women were perfectly capable of holding office and encouraged them to run, but she was willing to go no further on their behalf. Instead, she stuck to her principles of dealing with the needs of her family first and then those of the state of Wyoming.

Governor Nellie Ross continued to contend with the deep interest expressed in her by national women's organizations and by the press. She realized that her career was a milestone in the battle for women's equality. She was still enough of a believer in the traditional role of women, however, that when she addressed a group of Girl Scouts in 1925, she said, "I am old-fashioned enough to believe that no career for women is as glorious or satisfying as that which wifehood and motherhood offers, and it is there she fulfills her highest destiny." When asked later about her governorship, she said, "The best thing I could do for the women's cause at the time was to do a good as job as governor and afterwards. I wanted to show that women could take the responsibility and do well."

In the realm of politics, Nellie had to swim against the current. The people of Wyoming had rejected the Severance Tax Amendment to the constitution passed by her husband earlier in 1924, and both houses of the Wyoming legislature were dominated by Republicans. True to her word, she continued her husband's efforts to implement spending cuts, get state loans for agriculture, support Prohibition, regulate Wyoming banks and get more money for the University of Wyoming. Of the eleven proposals she offered, only five were accepted and acted upon by the legislature. Her proudest achievement was enacting a law compelling the use of safety devices in coal mines and more thorough and frequent inspections of mines, as Wyoming had suffered a string of disasters while her husband was still alive. Among her greatest challenges were the ongoing battles to enforce Prohibition, particularly in the northern part of the state and in Natrona County.

Another challenge for Governor Ross was with the federal government concerning the Rockefellers' desire to turn a substantial portion of their land near the Teton Mountains into another national park. She backed

*Left*: Nellie Tayloe Ross, the governor of Wyoming from 1925 to 1927. She was the first woman governor in Wyoming and the nation. *Wyoming State Archives, Department of State Parks and Cultural Resources.*

*Right*: Wyoming governor Nellie Tayloe Ross was honored with a bronze sculpture in front of the historic governor's mansion in 2022. She resided at the mansion during her husband's term and as governor. The bronze sculptor is Guadalupe Barajas, and the donors are Dixie and Tom Roberts. *Starley Talbott photograph.*

the concerns of many of Wyoming's citizens that the federal government already owned more than 50 percent of Wyoming's land and should not arbitrarily take any more.

Being busier than ever with her executive responsibilities, Nellie endeavored to continue her family's tradition of lavish entertainment at the governor's mansion. She frequently found herself unable to help with the preparations as she had before and was often late to her own parties. Fortunately, the women of Cheyenne came to her aid by greeting and entertaining guests until she could arrive.

At the end of her term in 1926, Nellie again ran for office but was defeated by Republican Frank Emerson. When asked why this happened, she stated that "she was a Democrat in a Republican state." For Republicans, there was fear that should she win, she would replace Francis E. Warren on the occasion of his retirement and become one of Wyoming's United States senators. It was also likely that she, like almost every Wyoming governor through the 1920s, could manage only one term thanks to the dreadful state of the economy. The people of Wyoming also had a political tradition in which governors usually served only one term, and it was a rare occasion in which anyone was offered a second term.

After her defeat, Nellie went on the speaking circuit, giving many lectures throughout Chautauqua, and she wrote many articles that were published in national magazines. She also continued to be very active in politics, this time on a national scale. Prior to her defeat in the governor's race, she attended the National Governor's Conference in Atlantic City, New Jersey. The possibility of her running for vice-president along with Al Smith was broached. She dismissed the opportunity out of hand, yet others were taking it seriously.

In 1928, Nellie was appointed one of the five vice-chairmen of the Democratic National Committee and as head of the women's division of the party. She engaged in widespread speaking tours that took her from Florida to Minnesota on behalf of the party. When the Democratic National Convention convened in Houston, Texas, she was surprised that the Wyoming convention had endorsed Al Smith with her as his vice-president. Ignoring the placards advocating for her, she commented, "I am here to work for Governor Smith and for the success of the principles of the Democratic Party." She got her wish and received only 25 of the 1,099 votes cast.

Nellie continued to cochair the Democratic National Committee, and in the 1932 election, she hit the campaign trail again, this time to mobilize the "the potential woman power of the party" as she toured the western states on behalf of Franklin Delano Roosevelt. She urged men to allow women to participate in government, not as auxiliaries to male power, but as a political force of their own.

Following his election for president, Franklin Delano Roosevelt appointed Nellie Tayloe Ross the first woman director of the United States Mint in 1933. She ran the mint as an efficient and humane executive for the next twenty years.

The mint's operations were huge and included the facilities in Philadelphia and Denver and the assay offices in Seattle and New York City. Nellie's responsibilities expanded when she had a direct hand in the creation of the national depositories at Fort Knox and West Point and the mint at San Francisco. All three bear her name on their cornerstones. For the U.S. Mint personnel she oversaw, she immediately implemented a program of accountability. In this program, all employees were fingerprinted and had their backgrounds checked by the Secret Service. She insisted that everyone who worked at the mint must have a perfect record. For new technologies implemented by the mint, she oversaw the installation of new presses that could strike two coins at the same time.

Throughout the most difficult years in the U.S. Mint's history—namely, the Great Depression and World War II—Nellie managed the mint effectively. She continued as the director of the mint through the Roosevelt and Truman administrations. In all the projects and challenges she faced, she leaned on her sense of economy in running the administration and frequently asked Congress for less money than they had allotted. When asked to account for the gold at Fort Knox, she assured Congress that it was all there—and it was. In all, Nellie developed a well-deserved reputation in Washington as a very efficient and pain-staking executive. When Dwight Eisenhower became president, Nellie attempted to resign, but he insisted that she stay on through the rest of her term, which concluded in 1953.

Nellie Tayloe Ross retired as director of the U.S. Mint with an enviable record. In 1953, the mint was operating with fewer people than it had been in the 1930s but was striking as much as four times the number of coins. The cost for doing so had risen 70 percent since the end of World War II, yet she was able to reduce the mint's expenses by 26 percent.

Upon her retirement, Nellie Tayloe Ross remained at her home in Washington, D.C. She returned to Wyoming often, and she made strong efforts to keep in touch with developments there both socially and politically. Nellie Tayloe Ross died on December 19, 1977, at the age of 101, and was buried beside her husband in Lakeview Cemetery.

# 20

# ELIAS WHITCOMB

## *Cowboy Hall of Famer*

Elias Whitcomb lived a life of adventure from his birth in 1833 to his death in 1915. His many achievements as a western pioneer earned him an honored place in the Cowboy Hall of Fame.

Whitcomb was born in Massachusetts, and by the age of twenty-four, he had arrived in Missouri, where he became a driver of a wagon pulled by oxen carrying consumer goods to markets in New Mexico. From there, he went to Leavenworth, Kansas, where he met Hiram Kelly and teamed up with Kelly to transport merchandise and herds of cattle to Fort Laramie, Wyoming.

Kelly and Whitcomb remained lifelong friends after arriving in Wyoming in 1857. Whitcomb soon established himself as a trader and eventually founded the Whitcomb and Cowgill Dry Goods Store in Cheyenne.

Eventually, Whitcomb established several ranching operations in Wyoming. He purchased land in southeastern Wyoming in the 1880s that became the Whitcomb Ranch near Chugwater, which he sold to the Swan Land and Cattle Company. He also owned land in northern Wyoming along the Belle Fourche River near Devils Tower. At one time, Whitcomb and Hiram Kelly also had ties to the Fort Collins, Colorado area.

On February 15, 1865, Elias Whitcomb married Katherine Shaw. She was the daughter of a Scottish man who was a trader and a woman from the Sioux Nation of Natives. In 1868, the couple built an impressive home on Carey Avenue in Cheyenne. It is said that Kate had a difficult time adjusting to her husband's culture, and she left him in Cheyenne to return to her tribe

Elias Whitcomb with his son Harold. *Wyoming State Archives, Department of State Parks and Cultural Resources.*

in the Fort Laramie area. She was persuaded to return to Cheyenne, where Elias hired a tutor to educate Kate and their children. They were the parents of Elizabeth Whitcomb Badgette, May Whitcomb Hume, Ida Whitcomb Schnitger and Harold Miller Whitcomb.

The Whitcombs became prominent citizens of Wyoming's capital city in Cheyenne. Their neighbors included many of Cheyenne's pioneer leaders, including their friends, Hiram "Hi" Kelly and his family. Kelly had married Elizabeth Richard, the daughter of a Fort Laramie trader and a woman who was also from the Sioux Nation of Natives.

A portrait of Kate Whitcomb, circa 1875. *Wyoming State Archives, Department of State Parks and Cultural Resources.*

In addition to his life in Cheyenne, Elias spent a good deal of time at his Belle Fourche Ranch in northern Wyoming. He was said to be an exceptionally fine horseback rider and spent much of his time riding the rangeland. He was killed by lightning while riding a favorite horse Ship Wheel at his ranch near Devil's Tower on June 15, 1915.

Some of Elias Whitcomb's amazing adventures in the American West were recorded in a transcript from the Works Progress Administration Collection compiled in the 1930s. A portion of Whitcomb's unpublished diary appeared in a 1906 interview with the Whitcomb family. The following are a few excerpts from that interview:

*I left Westport, Missouri, the middle of May 1857, having entered the employ of Childs brothers to drive an ox team to the then unknown region of New Mexico. The trip covered from May until the last of August. Our train contained about twenty wagons and twenty-three men. Buffalo covered the plains, myriads of them. We estimated that at a single view, we could see a hundred thousand.*

*We returned to Leavenworth, Kansas, which was at that time a military post and general western outfitting point. We loaded with freight for Fort Laramie, where Hiram Kelly joined the mule train. That fall was extremely rainy, and our progress was slow. We plodded along over rough trails and arrived at Fort Laramie on November 7. We spent the winter at Fort Laramie and left there on April 28, 1858, for Fort Douglas in Utah. We encountered terrible road conditions and reached Fort Douglas*

Elias Whitcomb driving a team of horses past his home in Cheyenne near the Wyoming State Capitol on December 25, 1899. *Wyoming State Archives, Department of State Parks and Cultural Resources.*

*in June. We immediately returned to Leavenworth, arriving in August, and started a second trip to Fort Laramie.*

*I passed the second winter in Fort Laramie. In 1859, I was placed in charge of all work cattle, about twelve hundred scattered up and down several creeks in the area. Antelope were very numerous. Our principal meat was antelope and deer. During the summer of 1859, there was quite a heavy emigration of people whose destination was California, Oregon or Washington. At this time, I severed my connection with the freighting company and entered the trading business on my own account.*

*In the spring of 1861, I moved to Horse Shoe Creek, where I operated a trading store, having a stock of groceries, liquors, and a few articles of clothing. Trouble happened when some of my enemies in the trading business burned my house and store to the ground.*

*By 1865, I moved to Fort Halleck. The following year, in the fall of 1865, I moved to the Cache La Poudre area near Fort Collins, Colorado. I bought twelve thousand pounds of potatoes at seven cents a pound and hauled the potatoes to Fort Laramie to sell. I also hauled wood for the government at ten dollars a day while there.*

Unfortunately, Whitcomb's diary concluded sometime in 1866. The whereabouts of the original document or any additional transcripts are unknown.

In 1971, Elias Whitcomb was inducted into what was then called the Cowboy Hall of Fame in Oklahoma City, Oklahoma. The May 14, 1971 edition of the *Moorcroft Leader* newspaper included this description of the honor:

> *Mr. Whitcomb was a man who possessed all of the traits most desired in the character of the men who pioneered the American West; a cattleman whose life experienced fighting Indians and sophisticated living in a mansion on Cheyenne's Cattlemen's Row.*

The National Cowboy and Western Heritage Museum was founded in 1955 and collects, preserves and exhibits an internationally renowned collection of western art and artifacts. The museum honors the men and women who have, through their exemplary lives, careers and achievements, embodied and perpetuated the heritage of the American West through its

The Whitcomb family monument in Lakeview Cemetery. *Starley Talbott photograph.*

three halls of fame. They include the Hall of Great Westerners, the Hall of Great Western Performers and the Rodeo Hall of Fame.

A photograph and description of the life of Elias Whitcomb now resides in the section of the museum known at the Hall of Great Westerners. He was buried in Lakeview Cemetery along with other family members.

21

# FRANK COLLINS EMERSON

## *Water for the West*

As a young civil engineer, Frank Emerson was drawn to the West, where there was ample opportunity to engage in extensive irrigation projects over newly reclaimed lands. He arrived in northern Wyoming in 1904 at the small hamlet of Cora. There, he took up management of the small mercantile and post office that served the many small farmsteads that were being built in the area. He traded his suit for a six-gallon hat and frequently rode horseback fifty miles to attend "break down" dances, the only entertainment for miles.

Emerson was born on May 26, 1882, in Saginaw, Michigan. His father was a painter and grainer, a specialist in painting faux knotholes and wood grain on door jambs and window frames. Frank was educated in the public schools of Saginaw, but baseball and swimming were his favorite activities. He graduated from the University of Michigan with a bachelor of science degree in civil engineering.

Upon his arrival in Wyoming, Emerson quickly engaged in the irrigation projects in the region and put his efforts as a civil engineer to work. He served for a time as the engineer for the La Prele Irrigation Project and then advanced to become the chief engineer for the Wyoming Land and Irrigation Company, overseeing its construction between 1908 and 1910.

Emerson also became the superintendent of the Big Horn Canal, the Lower Hanover Canal Association and the Wyoming Sugar Company, eventually serving in all capacities simultaneously. In order to supervise these operations, he first moved to Greybull and then to Worland, where he also worked for the Worland Drainage District. In his spare time, he became president of the Farmer's Cooperative Lumber Company of Worland and owned several farms and homes.

On January 17, 1910, he married his longtime sweetheart Sennia Jean Reynders, whom he had met in college. The couple became the parents of three sons, Frank Jr., David and Eugene.

Among his many endeavors, Frank worked for several months with the Wyoming State Engineering Department in 1905. His reputation was solidly established there, and when, in 1919, James B. True resigned his position, Governor Robert D. Carey selected Emerson to be his replacement.

Emerson moved to Cheyenne in July and quickly settled into his role. Water had been a principal concern of the State Engineers Office for more than a decade. Thousands of acres had been reclaimed across Wyoming thanks to the 1896 Carey Act, and Emerson was intimately knowledgeable of the many new canals and reservoirs that had been built across the state. It was also a timely appointment, as the state was experiencing a terrible drought, and the management of water was increasingly critical. Emerson began touring the countryside, examining the state's water resources. He made it publicly known that measuring devices were to be placed at the headgates of canals and reservoirs, public and private, to ensure that only the legal amount of water was being stored and used. This also necessitated him taking on the difficult questions regarding water usage rights, for which the new instruments would prove to be invaluable.

On an even grander scale, Emerson was employed by Governor Carey to engage with neighboring states and the federal government to manage shared water resources. Colorado and Wyoming had past disputes over water, and Wyoming had secured an injunction to keep farmers in northern Colorado from diverting Wyoming's water for their purposes. At the federal level, there were great concerns about the waters of the North Platte and Snake Rivers, which were shared by Nebraska, Idaho and various interested entities downstream. Also, there were numerous projects within Wyoming of the United States Bureau of Reclamation that had to be overseen to see that Wyoming's water interests were considered. Emerson frequently found himself dispatched to Denver and Washington to discuss these issues, and while in Wyoming, he made careful surveys of water resources, looking for any opportunity to advance opportunity for reclamation.

In 1921, Emerson struck on a plan to dam the North Platte River at Alcova, Wyoming. The intent was to create a stable water supply capable of irrigating 125,000 acres of land north and west of Casper. The dam needed to be 125 feet high, as it would also provide hydroelectric power for the region. After surveying the project himself, Emerson and the State of Wyoming engaged the federal government for help, as it would be far too expensive, at $2 million, for the state to manage on its own. Arthur P. Davis of the Reclamation Bureau was impressed by the proposal and asked Emerson to come to Washington to explain the project. It would take time for the details of the project to be implemented. Construction was eventually authorized in 1933 by President Franklin Roosevelt.

In 1922, Emerson was again involved with a major irrigation project, the largest of his lifetime. For years, seven states had been wrangling with the issue of what to do with the waters of the mighty Colorado River. California was growing explosively, with Arizona close behind. Upstream, the states of New Mexico, Utah and Colorado also wanted to use the water for their growth. Wyoming, too, had designs on its waters, as the Green River was one of its main feeding tributaries. With so many states involved, the federal government established a commission to settle water use issues and begin collective reclamation projects under the guidance of Secretary of Commerce Herbert Hoover. The resulting project was fantastically ambitious and resulted in the largest irrigation project ever attempted. At the estimated cost of $600 million, the project would irrigate five million acres of land and would require the construction of a gigantic dam in the Boulder Canyon, 150 miles north of Yuma, Arizona. This enormous structure (which would eventually be known as the Hoover Dam) became the tallest concrete structure ever attempted and would generate six million horsepower in electricity generation.

Wyoming had cause to be alarmed. In 1903, the brand-new U.S. Bureau of Reclamation was authorized to begin construction of the massive Pathfinder Dam on the North Platte west of Casper. The people of Wyoming had been promised that water from the project would be used to irrigate large portions of Wyoming. By 1922, however, the water that had been stored by the project was actually earmarked for the sole use of Nebraska. Mindful of the potential for disaster for Wyoming, Emerson went to Washington in January. Emerson became an integral part of the discussion, and he, along with W.F. McClure of California, was given the responsibility to measure the volume of water in the Colorado River, with and without storage facilities. Wyoming's newspaper editors gave Emerson full credit for representing the state and being wide awake to the potential dangers for the state. Just the same, he urged the people of Wyoming to be willing to compromise. If the state was too radical in its demands, there would be no agreement. He instead thought that there would be a fair reciprocity between all the states.

In April, Herbert Hoover stated, "No one need have any fear that any act of the commission will countenance diversion of water to the detriment of a single acre of Wyoming land. Should the matter get into the courts, the problem may become serious, but if an amicable settlement can be arrived at, it will be found. I am firmly of the belief that there is plenty of water to meet the demands of all."

On November 24, 1922, Frank Emerson was one of the signatories of the Colorado River Compact, allotting each state to a share of the water and a framework for its management for years to come. It was a milestone achievement; never before had so many states signed an agreement for their collective benefit over the West's waters.

As 1923 dawned, Robert D. Carey was replaced by William B. Ross as Wyoming's governor. Emerson had been appointed by Carey in 1919, but his position had not been officially confirmed by the senate. To correct this, Emerson sent his commission to the 1923 legislature, and the senate did approve it, but Ross did not officially submit the commission for such approval. Ross sent this letter to Emerson:

> *By your failure to observe the proper respect that is due to the office of governor, you have destroyed your usefulness as a public officer and made it wholly impossible for you and the executive to work in harmony. The establishment of such a precedent as this would tend to destroy the efficiency of the government by leading other appointive officers to seek similar devious methods prejudicial to the welfare of the state of retaining office regardless of the wishes of the appointive power.*

Emerson said that he had been legally appointed and would hold office until the courts decided against him. He was forcibly removed from his office on March 15 by the Laramie County sheriff. The district court eventually restored Emerson to his position, as he successfully argued that he could be removed from his six-year term in office only for cause.

In 1925, on the last day of the session, the Wyoming legislature killed its provisional approval of the Colorado River Compact. Emerson personally prevailed upon the leaders of the legislature, against the wishes of his own party leaders, to stop the clock, suspend the rules and continue meeting through Sunday and the following Monday to pass a new ratification bill, thus saving Wyoming's participation in that vital project. Emerson's supporters believed this was his greatest political triumph, and whispers began to circulate that he should be governor.

In the elections of 1926, Emerson ran against William Ross's wife, Nellie Tayloe Ross, as a Republican for the governorship of Wyoming. Francis E. Warren, the venerable octogenarian representing Wyoming in the United States Senate gave his hearty endorsement to Emerson:

> *I am firmly convinced that Frank Emerson as governor will be exactly the right man in the right place at this time. He seems to be the man of the hour, and in my opinion, he can best serve, safeguard and protect all of the varied interests of our state. I know him well and most favorably. He is an earnest worker, possesses a keen business mind, and has had the right kind of experience and training for the work at hand.*
>
> *Wyoming is no longer a broad expanse of sheep and cattle ranges only. Our vast, undeveloped resources are now our chief concern. They must be conserved, protected and brought to the attention of the world for development purposes....Whom can we name more competent to fulfill this great work, this solemn trust, than Frank Emerson?...A choice has been made, and Frank Emerson has been selected. He is in every way well fitted for the achievement of what Wyoming needs most—a progressive realization of the wealth of our state, its lands, its minerals, and its irrigation and waterpower possibilities. The people of Wyoming will take a distinctive step forward in choosing Frank Emerson to head their state government.*

In an unusual observation, newspapers witnessed that Brad Ross and Eugene Emerson were campaigning for their parents, handing out stickers and shaking hands with well-wishers. Both young men went to school together and had been on the same football team. Aside from this heartwarming episode, the election was a bitter one. Frank Emerson defeated Mrs. Ross by only 1,200 votes and was sworn into office in 1927.

Both houses of the Wyoming legislature were dominated by Republicans. Emerson promised that he would attempt to bring industry and mineral development to the state, but he was unable to do so. The economy of the state was heavily damaged by years of financial hardship, and attempts to bring more benefits to Wyoming through its mining industry proved fruitless.

Emerson turned his attentions instead to what he knew best: reclamation of Wyoming's water resources. Unfortunately, he ran afoul of the federal government's reticence to start any new projects in the state due to the

Frank Emerson, the governor of Wyoming from 1927 to 1931, at the governor's desk in the Wyoming State Capitol. *Wyoming State Archives, Department of State Parks and Cultural Resources.*

effects of the Great Depression. What he did do was to rigorously defend Wyoming's water rights on the North Platte and Green Rivers.

Other matters during Emerson's administration also proved difficult. He intended to expand the state's highway system to reach areas not touched by the main arteries. These efforts were difficult, as the established main highways absorbed much of the available federal funds and local tax revenue. The ability of the state to fund all of its obligations was also strained; as enrollment at the University of Wyoming increased, so did the number of patients at the dozen state hospitals. To help raise the funds, Emerson tried and failed to convince the Wyoming legislature to expand taxation on private property. The efficient management of the budget was vital in Emerson's eyes. He rigorously enforced foreclosures on farms that had forfeited on state loans and, at the same time, fought to increase the number of loans and reasonable terms for farmers still struggling in Wyoming's hinterland.

Despite Emerson's considerable difficulties in his first term in office, the people of Wyoming granted Emerson a second term in the elections of 1930 over his Democratic challenger, Leslie Miller of Cheyenne. Former governor Fenimore Chatterton offered these remarks about Emerson at his second inauguration:

> *Governor Emerson has given the state four years of hottest, efficient, constructive and economical administration, which, by reason of experience gained, is assurance of further and greater accomplishment for the wellbeing of Wyoming, for its advancement in material development and for its continued and increasing influence in the affairs of the nation.*

During the 1931 legislature, Emerson tried to convince the Wyoming solons that it was necessary to establish a state income tax. This endeavor predictably failed. It was to be one of the last fights he had in that august body. He had not been feeling well for several weeks, and doctors were concerned that he had exhausted himself with the election and the preparations for the legislature.

Emerson disregarded the doctors' orders to rest and contracted a case of the flu in mid-February. This infection rapidly developed into a severe case of pneumonia, which claimed his life on February 18, 1931. An outpouring of grief followed Emerson's untimely death. Seventeen cannons, fired at Fort Warren in his honor, could be heard throughout the city as he was interred at Lakeview Cemetery.

# 22

# EARL VANDEHEI

## *Horses, Dogs and Water*

An unusual monument honors the life of Earl Vandehei. It is dedicated to the special place that horses occupied for most of Earl's remarkable life.

Born in Harrison, Wisconsin, on May 15, 1896, Earl was the child of Peter and Emma Vandehei. Earl's mother died when he was only four years old. In 1912, Earl traveled with his father to investigate homesteading opportunities in Wyoming. Peter drove a wagon pulled by horses, and Earl rode his pony Gypsy to the Bear Creek area in Goshen County, Wyoming.

Father and son arrived in Wyoming with thirteen head of cattle and a few personal possessions. Peter Vandehei constructed a small house on 320 acres he acquired through the Enlarged Homestead Act of 1909. This act provided land to farmers who accepted marginal lands. Life on the small homestead was difficult for Peter and Earl. While his father worked at the homestead, Earl found employment on nearby ranches, performing chores like splitting wood, milking cows, harvesting hay and working to roundup livestock.

Earl was inducted into the United States Army in 1918 and served in France from July 1918 to June 1919. Peter died in 1919 while visiting family in Idaho. When Earl returned to the property on Bear Creek, he resumed ranching on his own while also working on other farms in the area. He was able to acquire additional acreage near the original homestead. When another parcel of land became available, Earl rode his horse for fifty miles from LaGrange, Wyoming, to Cheyenne during the night in order to be first in line at the government land office the next morning. He was successful in obtaining the land.

It was nothing for Earl to saddle up and ride his horse to a rodeo or a dance somewhere around Wyoming. He also enjoyed attending Cheyenne Frontier Days™ and became a lifelong supporter of the annual celebration. While still living in Goshen County, he would ride his horse to Cheyenne to see the parade and rodeo. His first stop would be to water his horse at the granite Humane Alliance Fountain at the corner of Fifteenth Street and Ferguson (now Carey) Avenue. The fountain stood at that location for many years, providing a drinking place for horses, dogs and other animals. It would later be moved to honor the man who was grateful for its existence.

During a rodeo and dance in Laramie, Wyoming, on July 4, 1923, Earl met his future wife, Flora Bowie. By the end of the summer, they were spending time together, riding in Earl's Model T Ford or riding horses on the prairie. They were engaged at Christmastime and married in August 1925. They lived in a house in downtown Cheyenne before acquiring a section of land north of Cheyenne on the old Yellowstone Highway.

By 1928, Earl and Flora had built a house on the property and a horse barn with a Dutch gamble roof. They eventually built or moved other buildings to the ranch. They settled into a busy life and raised a son, Gerald, and a daughter, Joy.

Earl had previously worked for a company that provided improvement to the streets in Cheyenne. He saw an opportunity to supply teams of horses to haul gravel and materials for the street projects. After successfully working with horse teams for various firms, Earl formed his own business, providing a horse-powered construction company.

As the business grew, Earl increased the number of teams and equipment necessary for his work. By the end of the 1920s, he had nearly one hundred horses drawing equipment. On large jobs, he often used as many as twelve teams, with a four-horse hitch on each team. He hired a full-time farrier to provide shoes for the horses.

During his long and successful career, Earl completed many projects almost exclusively with horse-drawn equipment. He was the grading contractor on Highway 85 from Cheyenne to Torrington, built runways at the Cheyenne Airport, dug numerous foundations for commercial and residential buildings and constructed a dam at the Wyoming Hereford Ranch near Cheyenne. In later years, his equipment was not horse-drawn, but he still found ways to utilize horses at every opportunity. He bred and sold horses to many customers, including the cavalry unit at Fort D.A. Russel (now F.E. Warren Air Force Base).

The Humane Alliance Fountain once stood at the intersection of Ferguson (Later Carey) Avenue and Fifteenth Street, providing a place for horses and dogs to find a drink of water. *J.E. Stimson Collection, Wyoming State Archives, Department of State Parks and Cultural Resources.*

Always a lover of horses, Earl raised Thoroughbreds and sought to improve the bloodlines of his animals. He entered his horses in races and jumping competitions throughout the West, where they often won contests as far away as Los Angeles, California.

As a lifelong fan of the Cheyenne rodeo, Earl especially enjoyed the racing events at Frontier Days. For years, he served as the "starter" for the horse races. He entered a team and wagon during the days when chuckwagon racing was an event at the annual celebration. Earl also rode with the Cheyenne polo team.

Even though horses were one of the highlights of Earl Vandehei's life, he was devoted to his family. His wife, Flora, was the bookkeeper for the business, completing chores like accounting for time on projects and preparing invoices. Earl and Flora celebrated life with their family, friends and many animals on the ranch. Their son, Gerald, and daughter, Joy, were also part of the family's work and recreational activities.

The ranch north of Cheyenne eventually became the home of Joy Vandehei, her husband, Tom Kilty, and their children, Kevin, Kerry, Deidre and Quinn. Gerald Vandehei and his family, Stephen, Richard, Kenneth and Peter, were also part of the family group, though they resided elsewhere.

Joy and Deidre operated a business on the property under the name Bar X Garden and Gifts in the 1990s. Much of the pasture land became part of the housing developments of Vandehei Estates and the Bar X Ranch Subdivision. The Vandehei name appears on the interchange sign from Interstate Highway 25 to Vandehei Avenue north of Cheyenne.

Earl Vandehei died in 1964 and was buried at Lakeview Cemetery. His grave came to be marked with an unusual monument. Years earlier, Earl would water his horse at a fountain in downtown Cheyenne. More than one hundred of these granite fountains were placed in communities throughout the nation to provide fresh drinking water for horses, dogs, cats and people. The fountains were provided free of charge by the National Humane Alliance Foundation, as long as a city provided an appropriate site, water supply and maintenance. Cheyenne's fountain stood at the corner of Fifteenth Street and Ferguson (now Carey) Avenue for many years but was moved to a different location at some point.

Earl Vandehei's grandson Steve said his grandfather always had a knack for being in the right place at the right time. Earl learned that city workers planned to demolish the fountain, so he offered to buy the fountain for $250 and asked the city crew to take the fountain to his ranch north of Cheyenne, where it remained for many years.

A portion of the Humane Alliance Fountain was moved to Lakeview Cemetery as the final resting place of Earl Vandehei, a rancher who used to ride his horse to Cheyenne and water the animal at the fountain. *Starley Talbott photograph.*

Eventually, the family moved the fountain to Lakeview Cemetery, where it stands as a fitting memorial to the man who loved horses. The granite piece above the water bowl was replaced with a replica engraved with the Vandehei name, marking Earl and Flora's graves. Later, the name Kilty was added for Joy, her husband, Tom, and their son Kerry who were buried in the family plot. The original capstone remains on the Lakeview monument.

The original piece above the water bowl, minus the lion's head faucets, resides at the home of Vandehei's granddaughter Deidre Newman, who said, "The fountain had provided Earl Vandehei's horses with water and a rest after a long journey and now served to mark Earl and Flora's final resting place."

# 23

# JOY VANDEHEI KILTY

## *Miss Frontier*

J oy Vandehei, the daughter of Earl and Flora Vandehei, grew up on her parent's ranch north of Cheyenne. She lived her entire life at the top of the hill, which is now the corner of Vandehei Avenue and Yellowstone Road.

While growing up on a horse ranch, Joy watched her father, Earl, train and trade horses. She knew the history of the ranch well and often told entertaining stories about her colorful father and many other interesting characters.

Following her graduation from Cheyenne High School in 1948, Joy attended the University of Wyoming, where she studied art. Her favorite subject was the American West, and she painted Western and Southwestern landscapes. Joy was an active member of Kappa Kappa Gamma Sorority, and she was selected as the Kappa Sigma Dream Girl by songwriter Hoagie Carmichael.

In 1949, Joy was selected to represent Cheyenne Frontier Days™ as the lady-in-waiting and then as Miss Frontier in 1950. Her father provided Joy and her lady-in-waiting, Laura Bailey, with matching Palomino horses for the parades and matching white Pinto horses to ride at the rodeo. During her reign as rodeo royalty, Joy wore the traditional custom-made white buckskin split skirt with a vest and white silk shirt. One of her fondest memories of the 1950 celebration was meeting the Oglala Sioux woman named Princess Blue Water.

*Right*: Joy Vandehei, the daughter of Earl and Flora Vandehei, grew up on a ranch north of Cheyenne. She attended the University of Wyoming and was selected as lady-in-waiting in 1949, advancing to Miss Frontier in 1950. She married Tom Kilty, and the couple resided in Cheyenne, where she was involved with many civic interests. *Cheyenne Frontier Days™ Old West Museum photograph.*

*Below*: Miss Frontier Joy Vandehei *(left)* and Lady-in-Waiting Laura Bailey pose with matching horses provided by Earl Vandehei for use while promoting Cheyenne Frontier Days™. *Wyoming State Archives, Department of State Parks and Cultural Resources.*

When the Cheyenne Frontier Days™ Old West Museum was established in 1978, Joy and her mother, Flora, donated carriages and memorabilia to the museum. Joy's daughter Deidre had the honor of representing the annual celebration as Miss Frontier in 1978. It was the first time the daughter of a former queen was crowned. Joy's father, Earl, and members of the family were inducted into the Cheyenne Frontier Days™ Hall of Fame in 2013.

Following Joy's involvement as queen of the rodeo, she married Tom Kilty. The couple resided near the original family ranch north of Cheyenne. Joy was involved with many civic interests, including the Cheyenne Women's Civic League, the Hospital Auxiliary, the Questers Antique Club and the Kappa Kappa Gamma alumni group. Joy and Tom became the parents of four children, Kevin, Kerry, Deidre and Quinn.

During the 1980s and 1990s, Joy and Tom developed much of the land they owned into what became the North Forty subdivision and the Bar X Ranch subdivision. Joy and her daughter Deidre owned and operated the Bar X Garden and Gifts, an antique store and garden center located in the original Dutch gambrel barn at the Vandehei ranch.

Joy's daughter Deidre Kilty Newman said her mother was the epitome of the casual elegance that she admired about Wyoming, and she lived with passion and devotion to Western life. Joy died on June 3, 2009, and was buried near her parents, her husband, Tom, and their son Kerry at Lakeview Cemetery. The family's memorial marker is part of a historic granite water fountain that was moved from downtown Cheyenne to the ranch and later to the cemetery, where it has been included in many historic cemetery walks.

# 24

# WILLIAM HALE

## *Yellowstone Remains in Wyoming*

**W**yoming's fourth territorial governor, William Hale, arrived in Wyoming on August 22, 1882. He was nominated by President Chester A. Arthur and was confirmed unanimously by congress. He is best known for developing Wyoming's mining potential and for his involvement in regulations within the nation's first national park, Yellowstone.

Hale was born in Henry County, Iowa, on November 18, 1837. When he was four years old, the family moved to Oskaloosa, Iowa, where his father died. He was raised on the family farm until he was sixteen years of age, when he became an apprentice carpenter. He trained for three years and subsequently earned a good reputation as a mechanic. Not content with the trades, he enrolled at William Penn University in Oskaloosa, where he studied law.

After Hale earned a law degree in 1858, he moved to Mills County, Iowa, in the town of Glenwood, where he set up a practice with his longtime partner E.P. Stone. Together, the men developed a formidable practice that became one of the most respected in the state. In 1864, Hale was elected to the Iowa legislature and was reelected in 1868. A lifelong Republican, Hale advanced his party's platform both locally and nationally, campaigning on Ulysses S. Grant's behalf throughout the state in 1868.

In 1866, Hale married Francis E. Rounds of Oskaloosa, and together, they had three sons. In 1880, he was struck by Addison's disease, a condition that would eventually take his life. Seeking improvements for his health, he

William Hale, the territorial governor of Wyoming from 1882 to 1885, is honored with this monument in Lakeview Cemetery. *Starley Talbott photograph.*

temporarily moved to Hawaii, where he met the king and queen of the islands personally.

Following his return from Hawaii, Hale made his first camping trip to Colorado in 1881. He became interested in a Colorado mine in 1882 and came out west to manage the mine's affairs personally. Iowa citizens praised Hale when, on July 19, 1882, President Chester A. Arthur nominated him to be the governor of Wyoming Territory.

Following his arrival in Cheyenne, Hale quickly proved himself to be a stable and excellent executive. When his health permitted it, he was energetic in developing Wyoming's mining potential.

During Hale's term in Wyoming, one of the most contentious issues was in regard to the operation of the law in Yellowstone National Park. Growing ever more concerned with hotel interests, poaching and other potential criminal behavior, the Territories of Montana, Idaho and Wyoming attempted to establish the primacy of their laws within the park. Hale stridently opposed efforts by Montana governor John Schuyler Crosby to impose Montana game regulations within the park. He was aided by Wyoming newspapers that were scandalized when Governor Crosby reported that Yellowstone was located in Montana. Hale sent a letter to the United States Senate in February 1883, protesting the interference of the governor of Montana. Crosby responded by sending a letter to Governor Hale. Eventually, the conflict was resolved, and Yellowstone Park remained in Wyoming under the guidance of Wyoming laws.

Hale was well liked by the citizens of Wyoming Territory, and they followed stories of his continuing decline with concern. In 1883, Hale returned to Iowa to convalesce at Glenwood Springs. After returning to Wyoming in 1884, Hale was sufficiently weakened by his disease and needed to be propped up by pillows in his carriage while working on the campaign trail. On January 10, 1885, he was struck again with a severe bout of the disease and was rendered unconscious. He died at his home on Eighteenth Street in Cheyenne on January 14, 1885, becoming the first governor of Wyoming to die while in office. Hale was buried in Lakeview Cemetery.

# 25

# JIM "KIDD" WILLOUGHBY

## *Cowboy*

A small marker at Lakeview Cemetery identifies one of the famous cowboys from the early days of Wyoming as "Cowboy." Though he was born Jim Willoughby on September 17, 1857, in Missouri, the gravestone states his name was "Jim Kidd."

Willoughby was a rider for several southeastern Wyoming ranchers in the late 1800s. He joined the *Buffalo Bill Wild West Show* in 1885. He also worked with the Forepaugh Circus and Cole Younger and Frank James Wild West shows. Sometime during these adventures, he was dubbed with the name "Kidd" or "Kid."

Around 1913, Kid moved to California and played minor roles and acted as a stuntman in Hollywood. Harry Gant, a cameraman, said Jim Kid was among the first real cowhands who came to Hollywood as a stuntman. Kid also made many friends among the movie stars in Hollywood, including Douglas Fairbanks.

On December 11, 1916, Jim Kid died after a riding accident in one of his films. He had told a friend that if he died, he wished to be buried in Cheyenne. A group of his Hollywood friends planned to take up a collection to send the Kid's body to Cheyenne for burial, but Douglas Fairbanks agreed to pay for all the expenses to grant Kid's final wish. Kid was honored with a cowboy funeral in Hollywood, and a large group of friends accompanied his body to the train depot to send the cowboy back to his hometown in Cheyenne.

Jim Kidd Willoughby's Wild West photograph. *Wyoming State Archives, Department of State Parks and Cultural Resources.*

The following account of the Hollywood services appeared in the *Los Angeles Examiner*:

> *Customs of frontier days, so dear to the hearts of the range rovers who insist upon their periodical rodeos and other reminiscent events, will not suffer a departure even in death. This was the will of Jim Kid, he was always plain Jim, and arrangements are now being made to administer the same last rides.*
>
> *A few years ago, the lure of the movies claimed Jim, and he saddled up his old sorrel horse and rode into town. At one of the studios at Hollywood, Jim Kidd made many thrillers for the screen. Jim was one of the most skillful riders in the ranks of the movie cowboys.*
>
> *Jim will be honored next Sunday from one of the Hollywood churches with the solemn rites observed by the range of folk of years ago. He will be borne in an antiquated hearse, drawn by four pinto horses, while a long column of his fellows will follow in the saddle, led by Jim's old horse with saddle reversed.*
>
> *The following well-known movie performers will act as pallbearers: Douglas Fairbanks, William Gettinger, Vestaer Pegg, Harry Carey, Fred Burns, Harry Burns, Harry Gant and Bud Osborne.*

The December 22, 1916 edition of the *Cheyenne State Leader* carried the following article:

> *Jim Kidd Laid at Rest Here: Last Solemn Rites for Old-Time Wyoming Cowboy Held Yesterday Afternoon*
>
> *The last chapter of the remarkable life of Jim "Kidd" Willoughby, pioneer Wyoming cowboy, was written in Cheyenne yesterday when he was buried here. A score of friends who knew him when he was riding the range a generation ago gathered at the undertaking.*
>
> *Willoughby had not lived in Cheyenne for years, but the old-timers had kept in touch with him in Los Angeles, where he was engaged as a motion picture actor, depicting wild-west days. The body arrived here Wednesday, following a funeral service in Los Angeles, where motion picture acquaintances gathered to pay their last respects.*
>
> *A frontier committee attended the funeral and service at the grave. Some of Willoughby's effects, relics of the early '80s in Wyoming, were carried in the cortege. They consisted of his saddle, bridle, chaps, stirrups, hat,*

Jim Kidd Willoughby "Cowboy" is honored with this headstone in Lakeview Cemetery from "his friends." *Starley Talbott photograph.*

*cartridge belt and Colt revolver. These mementos of days gone by will be presented to the Industrial Club.*

*The pallbearers were life-long friends, Percy Hoyt, George Gillard, Frank Meanes, Warren Richardson, Charles W. Hirsig and Harry Hynds.*

Close to a pathway in Lakeview Cemetery is the small monument marking Willoughby's grave, with the statement, "From His Friends." It is often adorned with fresh flowers left by unknown admirers.

# 26

# DAISY "DAZEE" McCABE BRISTOL

## *Cheyenne's Flower*

Much has been written of the life and times of Daisy McCabe, her birth name, but she came to be known in Cheyenne as "Dazee." Born on May 9, 1878, in Missouri, she moved to Cheyenne with her parents in 1892.

Dazee attended a convent school in North Platte, Nebraska, before moving to Cheyenne. She graduated from Cheyenne's Central High School in 1897. She taught school at Archer, east of Cheyenne, for a short time before she married Lieutenant Charles Bristol, a veteran of the Spanish-American War who was stationed at Fort D.A. Russell (later F.E. Warren Air Force Base). They were married in 1900 at the home of Dazee's parents.

The young bride quickly became the toast of the town, according to those who wrote about Dazee's varied life. She had been trained in music and drama, and she appeared in several productions at the Cheyenne Opera House. Dazee and Charles were active in social events in Cheyenne, and Dazee was known as an excellent dancer and a gracious hostess. The couple built a home at 720 East Twentieth Street in 1904. Charles became the vice-president of the S.A. Bristol Printing and Bindery Company, which was owned by his father. The company later became Pioneer Printing.

Described as a beautiful woman, Dazee was featured in a full-page photograph in *Redbook Magazine* in 1926. Her photograph also won a prize at the St. Louis World's Fair. She became known for her resplendent clothing and hats. In 1967, the Altrusa Club (one of the many clubs where she maintained membership) gave her a "Dazee" doll. The doll was a replica of Dazee dressed in her purple shawl and hat with a sweeping plume, a costume that had made her famous for years.

Though Dazee was known for her many special talents, she is perhaps best known for her work in the parades during Cheyenne Frontier Days™. Beginning in 1926, she created several floats for the parade, described in her own words:

> Prior to 1926, the Frontier Days Parades were very pathetic affairs that usually consisted of our city band, perhaps a few Sioux Indians imported for the occasion, and big Charlie Irwin, our popular stockman and cowboy, leading a group of yelling cowboys galloping down Capitol Avenue.
>
> One night in May of 1926, the Chamber of Commerce held a meeting to discuss the idea of a real Frontier Parade, worthy of the name, "Daddy of Them All," a slogan coined for publicizing Frontier Days. Mrs. Fred Boice and I were contacted by the committee to provide subjects for the parade. Mrs. Boice helped to procure historic carriages for the parade and worked tirelessly for years on the carriage section, one of the highlights of the parade.
>
> Members of the committee contacted me to work a floats section of the parade, since I had participated in the Food Conservation parade during the First World War and planned several beautiful floats for that event. They asked me to design floats typifying frontier life in Wyoming.
>
> I thought of the rowdy saloons and dance halls of early days and came up with the float I named Hells Half Acre. The name was suggested because early day Cheyenne had been called a Hell on Wheels town. The float featured an old fashioned bar, a keg of beer on tap, a corner card game, and girls in short skirts dancing with gamblers and cowboys of the era.

One of Dazee's most popular floats was *Hiram's Dance Hall*, which featured musicians and square dancers. Hiram Davidson, a famous square dance caller and fiddler, appeared on the floats for many years. After his death, the float was renamed as *Dazee's Dance Hall*. It was on this float that Dazee wore her famous purple shawl and plumed hat and played the pump organ for more than fifty years. Other floats designed by Dazee included *Silver Crown Mining*, *Placer Mining*, *The Blacksmith* and *The Vigilantes*. She was inducted into the Cheyenne Frontier Days™ Hall of Fame in 2002.

Some who knew Dazee often changed the words of a famous song to "Dazee, Dazee, give me your answer true," because in Cheyenne, Dazee was sometimes called the "flower of the community." She was so much a

*Left*: Dazee Bristol obtained fame in 1926, when she was featured in a full-page photograph in *Redbook* magazine. *Wyoming State Archives, Department of State Parks and Cultural Resources.*

*Below*: Dazee Bristol playing her piano in Cheyenne's annual parade. As a member of the Cheyenne Frontier Days™ Hall of Fame, she is credited with being a fierce advocate of the event. *Union Pacific Railroad Photograph, Wyoming State Archives, Department of State Parks and Cultural Resources.*

*Opposite*: Dazee Bristol was a writer for the *Wyoming Tribune* and the *Wyoming Stockman Farmer*. She was a charter member of Wyoming Press Women and was honored by the group for being the oldest working press woman in the nation in 1978 on her one hundredth birthday. *Wyoming State Archives, Division of State Parks and Cultural Resources.*

part of Cheyenne's society that admirers said, "Without her, much of the sparkle would be gone."

Life lost some of its sparkle for Dazee when both her mother and her husband died in 1927. She became a widow at the age of fifty. Along with her many other pursuits, Dazee turned to writing. She enrolled in a writing and advertising class at the University of Denver, which led to her becoming well known for her contributions to several newspapers.

"Touring the Shops with Dazee" appeared on May 3, 1928, in the *Wyoming Tribune* and was published there for many years. She visited local shops, wrote clever copy interspersed with bits of style and social lore, giving the women of Cheyenne expert advice on where to shop. Dazee also became the women's page editor for the *Wyoming Stockman Farmer* with a column titled "Household Corner."

Dazee's journalistic career brought her many accolades. She was a charter member of the Wyoming Press Women and won many press awards throughout her years as a columnist. She earned the National Women of Achievement title from the Wyoming Press Women in 1963 at the age of eighty-five.

Dazee also remained active in the community, helping to organize several service clubs, including Altrusa Club and Cheyenne Women's Club,

American Legion auxiliary, historical society and others. She also contributed to the formation of the Cheyenne Little Theatre Players group.

On Dazee's one hundredth birthday on May 9, 1978, Governor Ed Herschler declared the day "Dazee Bristol Day." The Wyoming Press Women presented Dazee with a plaque, honoring her for being the oldest working press woman in the nation. Hundreds of people attended the party, and the newspaper touted Dazee as an institution in Cheyenne and Wyoming.

Daisy "Dazee" Bristol died on October 2, 1983, at the age of 105. She was buried in Lakeview Cemetery beside her husband, Charles. The couple had no children. Perhaps that is why the grave of Cheyenne's daisy flower is marked with a simple metal plate at ground level.

# 27

# LAKEVIEW CEMETERY TOURS

## *History Comes to Life*

Wwe have touched only a small portion of the stories beneath the stones at Cheyenne's Historic Lakeview Cemetery. A visit to the cemetery office at 2501 Seymour Avenue will provide the reader with additional information, including a tour guide pamphlet.

## SELF-GUIDED TOURS

The self-guided tour introduces the famous and the not-so-famous people who rest in peace at the cemetery. Visitors are encouraged to look at cemetery markers not simply as mute stones but as works of art and commentaries on the lives of the people they represent.

Certain symbols are common and often seen on gravestones in many places. Some examples include lambs, which stand for modesty, humility or the fragility of a child; doves, which symbolize peace, innocence and the flight to heaven; and winged cherubs, which represent the link between the passage of time and immortality, as well as resurrection.

Flowers and plants may be sacred or secular: daisies represent youth and innocence; lily of the valley represents purity; and pansies are the symbol of remembrance. Sometimes, state or national flowers indicate a person's birthplace and ancestry. The intermingling of oak and ivy represents strength, honor, friendship and immortality. A sheaf of wheat represents the elderly. Grapes and vines represent the Eucharist of holy communion.

*Right*: This memorial in the shape of a dream catcher was placed in Lakeview Cemetery to honor the lives of Natives whose remains were moved to the cemetery. *Starley Talbott photograph.*

*Below*: The plaque explains the purpose of the Dream Catcher Memorial in honor of Natives. *Starley Talbott photograph.*

*Opposite*: The Cheyenne Angel Statue at Lakeview Cemetery provides a place of solace. Tiles in remembrance of loved ones have been placed on the wall near the statue. *Starley Talbott photograph.*

Cheyenne Angel

A Place of Love
and Healing

We invite all to leave
a white flower at its base

Other symbols representing the occupation of the deceased or other accomplishments achieved during their lifetime may be present. Take time to notice some of the more unusual grave markers. One of these is that of a "dream catcher," marking an area holding the remains of Natives who were moved from another location to Lakeview.

A large statue near the south border of the cemetery is the Cheyenne Angel Statue. This statue was placed in remembrance of loved ones, especially children, who died. Some visitors place a symbolic white rose at the statue as a tribute. An angel tile may also be placed on the wall near the statue in remembrance of a loved one.

The tour pamphlet tells a brief history of the efforts and deeds of some of the people who pioneered, homesteaded and worked hard to build the city of Cheyenne and the state of Wyoming.

Those who wish to take the historical tour of the cemetery are reminded that Lakeview Cemetery is fully operational. Visitors are asked to leave all plants and memorial items in place, to leave no litter and to be courteous of other visitors and funerals in progress.

# LIVING HISTORY WALKS

The Cheyenne Genealogical and Historical Society is the sponsor of an annual Living History Walk at Lakeview Cemetery. The tour is usually held during the summer months, and participants are asked to pay a nominal fee to partake of the live presentations portrayed by members of the society and other residents.

The Cheyenne Genealogical Society was formed in 1952 to encourage family history research and support the acquisition of research and reference materials. The name was changed in 2006 to Cheyenne Genealogical and Historical Society. The group encourages and supports cooperative programs with the Special Collections Department of the Laramie County Library, the Cheyenne Family History Center and other state and local entities.

Sharon Lass Field has been instrumental in organizing the Living History Walk for several years. She is a member of the genealogical society and the author of several history books about Cheyenne and Laramie County. Field served as the greeter of the 2023 Living History Walk. She presented a brief history of the cemetery before guests were invited to join the walk to be introduced to the actors portraying the lives of people who shaped Wyoming and the West.

Field was joined by narrators and hostesses Jan Scheidt and Sheryl Swilling. The following people represented historic Wyoming characters, who may be buried in Lakeview Cemetery or in nearby cemeteries:

Dan Lyon portrayed Japanese Joe; Keith Thomson played George Throstle; Mary Guthrie played Estelle Reel; Reverend Catherine Fitzhugh represented Lucy Phillips; Warren Appel portrayed John

Sharon Lass Field is shown during the 2022 Living History Walk at Lakeview Cemetery. *Starley Talbott photograph.*

Pershing Boulevard, looking east, with Lakeview Cemetery on the right. Archie Allison's dairy barn is on the hill to the east, 1931. *Wyoming State Archives, Division of State Parks and Cultural Resources.*

Pershing Boulevard, looking east, with Lakeview Cemetery on the right, 2022. *Starley Talbott photograph.*

"Portagee" Phillips; Peter Kisiel played Levi Powell; Joe Bryan played Jean "Frenchy" Cazaban; Kelli Cook portrayed Frances Irwin; Jo Butler played Kate Whitcomb; Shane Brown played John Milatzo; Judy Englehart portrayed Apple Annie; Dan Sisnero played an unknown cowboy; and Nathan Hurley represented Willie Nickell.

Those who participate in the self-guided tour or the Living History Walk at Lakeview Cemetery are invited to take a brief journey into the past to gain an appreciation for the history of Cheyenne and Wyoming.

# BIBLIOGRAPHY

Allyn, F.H. Unpublished diary from the Women's Ministry. First Baptist Church (Cheyenne, WY), 1923. Wyoming State Archives.

Amundson, Michael A. *Wyoming Revisited: Rephotographing the Scenes of Joseph E. Stimson*. Boulder, CO: University Press of Colorado, 2014.

Bell, Hisano. Email translation of Japanese Tombs. December 26, 2021.

*Big Horn County Rustler*. "New Irrigation Project." June 24, 1921, 5.

———. "Notice of Incorporation of Wyoming Irrigation Company." April 10, 1914, 5.

*Big Horn Sentinel*. "Traveling Under Difficulties." April 7, 1888, 3.

Birt, Mary Jo. "To Hold a More Brilliant Torch: Suffragist and Orator Theresa Jenkins." www.WyoHistory.org.

Bristol, Dazee Collection. Wyoming State Archives.

*Brush Tribune*. "Chas. Irwin Injured in Wyoming Car Wreck." March 22, 1934.

*Burlington Weekly Hawk-Eye*. "Wyoming's New Governor." July 27, 1882, 10.

Burroughs, John Rolfe. *Guardian of the Grasslands: The First Hundred Years of the Wyoming Stock Growers Association*. Cheyenne, WY: Pioneer Printing and Stationary Company, 1971.

*Carbon County Journal*. "Hugus & Chatterton." March 24, 1888.

———. "Legislative Committees." November 22, 1890, 3.

———. "Republican Ticket." October 27, 1888, 2.

Carey Family Papers: 1869–1978. Archives West.

Carey, Joseph Maull. Delaware Public Archives.

Carlisle, Bill Collection. File 2. Cheyenne Frontier Days™ Old West Museum.

*Casper Star Tribune.* "Abundance of Water Available for Casper Irrigation Plans." March 8, 1921, 10.

———. "Already Divided." September 9, 1922, 6.

———. "A Bad Policy." September 1, 1922, 6.

———. "Carey and Carter Victors at Polls." November 5, 1930, 1.

———. "Carey Flays New Deal in Address at Midwest." October 9, 1936, 1.

———. "Carey Formally Announces Candidacy for U.S. Senate." January 14, 1930, 1.

———. "Carey on Way to Washington." November 24, 1930, 1.

———. "Carey's Life Is Reviewed." November 2, 1930, 20.

———. "Cattle Business Here Began with Herd of 15,000 Trailed Here by CY Outfit." October 26, 1930, 15.

———. "Citizens of Wyoming United in Praising Fearless Leader Suddenly Removed by Death Wednesday." February 19, 1931, 1.

———. "Death Claims Senator Frances E. Warren." November 11, 1929, 1.

———. "Do You Want a Clean Government?" November 6, 1922, 7.

———. "Emerson Takes Office Monday at Noon Hour." January 2, 1927, 1.

———. "Governor Ross Is Dead." October 2, 1924, 1.

———. "Governor Emerson Dead: Death Last Night Comes After Rally." February 19, 1931, 2.

———. "Gov. W.B. Ross Answers Call." October 2, 1924, 4.

———. "Hay's Last Chance Shattered." November 16, 1922, 1.

———. "Joseph M. Carey, Former Governor of State, Dead." February 6, 1924, 1.

———. "Loyal Work for State Led Emerson to Governorship." February 19, 1931, 1.

———. "Many Contributions Made by Carey to the City of Casper." January 18, 1937, 1.

———. "Name of Post Officially Changed to Fort Warren." January 1, 1930, 1.

———. "Possibilities of Irrigation in Wyoming Development Were Recognized by Carey." January 18, 1937, 8.

———. "Republican Candidates Address Laramie Meeting." October 14, 1930, 3.

———. "Roosevelt Landslide Grows: Carey Concedes Election of Schwartz." November 4, 1936, 1.

———. "Ross' Election Credited to Natrona Republicans." November 11, 1922, 1.

———. "Ross' Lead in State Count Is Cut to 529." November 15, 1922, 1.

———. "To Mr. H.H. 'Harry' Schwartz." October 7, 1936, 6.

———. "Warren's Senate Service Was Longest in History." November 11, 1929, 1.

———. "Widow of Governor Emerson to be Offered State Post." February 20, 1931, 1.

———. "William B. Ross Will Head List of Demo Speakers Wednesday." October 28, 1922, 3.

———. "Wm. B. Ross." October 2, 1924, 1.

———. "Wm. B. Ross in Casper Address." November 2, 1922, 1.

Chatterton, Fenimore C. *Yesterday's Wyoming: The Intimate Memoirs of Fenimore C. Chatterton, Territorial Citizen, Governor, Builder.* Aurora, CO: Power River Publishers and Book Sellers, 1957.

Cheyenne Centennial Committee. *The Magic City of the Plains: Cheyenne 1867–1967.* Cheyenne, WY: 1967.

*Cheyenne Daily Leader.* "Able Address." July 17, 1902, 1.

———. "Big Combination of Sheep Growers." July 17, 1901, 3.

———. "Board Organizes." June 3, 1903.

———. "City Council Meeting." February 2, 1881, 4.

———. "Dr. Johnson Endorses Dr. Barber." November 15, 1903, 4.

———. "Funeral of Mrs. Warren." April 2, 1902, 4.

———. "Governor Barber." November 25, 1890, 2.

———. "The Great Park: A Protest from the Governor of Wyoming Sent to the Senate." February 10, 1883, 3.

———. "A Letter to Governor Crosby to Governor Hale." February 14, 1883, 3.

———. "A Man of the People." September 26, 1902, 3.

———. "Montana Wants the Park." February 3, 1883, 3.

———. "Mrs. Richards Dies." October 28, 1903, 4.

———. "New Cattle Company." October 29, 1903, 4.

———. "Reward." July 26, 1901, 2.

———. "Sample Republican Ballot." November 6, 1894, 2.

———. "Speech by Theresa A. Jenkins." July 24, 1890.

———. "Sweeping Democratic Victory in This County." November 5, 1908, 1.

*Cheyenne Daily Sun.* "Governor Hale Dead." January 14, 1885, 3.

———. "Louder Than Words." November 2, 1884, 2.

———. "New Fort Russell." November 1, 1884, 1.

———. "What He Has Done." November 1, 1884, 3.

*Cheyenne Daily Sun-Leader.* "About the Robbers." June 15, 1899, 4.

———. "Courage, Wisdom, Energy and Money." June 13, 1899, 4.

———. "Regulars Ordered." June 20, 1899, 4.

*Cheyenne State Leader.* "Able Candidate for Congress." October 18, 1910, 2.

———. "Dr. Amos W. Barber." June 23, 1915, 12.

———. "Dr. A.W. Barber, Former Wyoming Executive, Dies." June 20, 1915, 5.

———. "Dr. Barber Operated On." March 9, 1915, 5.

———. "Emerson to Become State Engineer of Wyoming This Date." July 1, 1919, 5.

———. "Governor Carey Takes Oath on Bible Used When Father Was Sworn in as Governor." January 7, 1919, 1.

———. "With State Candidates as Speakers Democratic Rally Is Big Success." October 30, 1910, 1.

———. "Wyoming Congressman Re-Elected by Reduced Vote." November 10, 1910, 4.

*Cheyenne Tribune.* "Charlie Irwin as Famous Western Cowboy, Showman." March 24, 1934.

Cummings, Kathryn Swim. *Esther Hobart Morris.* Glendo, WY: High Plains Press, 2019.

*Daily Record.* "Was with the U.S. Mint for 20 Years, Longer Than Any Previous Director." September 12, 1976, 59.

Davis, John W. "The Johnson County War: 1892 Invasion of Northern Wyoming." www.WyoHistory.org.

———. *Wyoming Range War: The Infamous Invasion of Johnson County.* Norman: University of Oklahoma Press, 2010.

*Dayton Daily News.* "Mrs. Ross, Mint Director, Is Proud of 20-Year Record." March 16, 1953, 5.

*Democratic Leader.* "Death of Governor Hale." January 14, 1885, 2.

———. "The Governor's End." January 14, 1885, 2.

*De Moines Register.* "Governor Hale." July 14, 1883, 3.

*Douglas Enterprise.* "Dies at Hospital at Advanced Age." October 19, 1915, 1.

Drake, Kerry. "Francis E. Warren: A Massachusetts Farm Boy Who Changed Wyoming." November 8, 2014. www.WyoHistory.org.

Ewig, Rick. *Cheyenne: A Sesquicentennial History.* San Antonio, TX: HPN Books, 2017.

———. "Did She Do That? Examining Esther Morris' Role in the Passage of the Suffrage Act." *Annals of Wyoming* 78, no. 1 (Winter 2006): 26–34.

Ewig, Rick, Linda Rollins and Betty Griffin. *Wyoming's Capitol*. Cheyenne: Wyoming State Press, 1987.

Feinberg, John D., and Ellen T. Ittelson. *Cheyenne's Historic Architecture*. Cheyenne, WY: Prepared for the Cheyenne-Laramie County Regional Planning Office, 1990.

Field, Sharon Lass, ed. *History of Cheyenne, Wyoming: Laramie County*. Vol 2. Raleigh, NC: Curtis Media Corporation, 1989.

Flynn, Shirley. *Let's Go! Let's Show! Let's Rodeo! The History of Cheyenne Frontier Days*. Cheyenne, WY: Wigwam Publishing Company LLC, 1996.

Friis, Jessica. *High Plains Arboretum*. Charleston, SC: Arcadia Publishing, 2021.

*Good Housekeeping*. "The Governor Lady." August 1927.

Hanesworth, Robert D. *Daddy of 'Em All: The Story of Cheyenne Frontier Days*. Cheyenne, WY: Flintlock Publishing Company, 1967.

Hedquist, Seth. "Mead, Elwood." *Iowa State University Biographical Dictionary*. https://isubios.pubpub.org.

Hein, Rebecca. "Still Unsolved: The 1911 Deaths of Edna Richards Jenkins and Thomas Jenkins." www.WyoHistory.org.

———. "Wyoming Ratifies the 19th Amendment." www.WyoHistory.org.

Henderson, Vivian. "Tribute to Dr. Barber." *Wyoming Semi-Weekly Tribune* 20, no. 42 (May 25, 1915): 4.

Irwin, C.B. Collection. Box 1, folders 9 and 23. Cheyenne Frontier Days™ Old West Museum.

*Jackson Sun*. "Twenty Years as Director of U.S. Mint Did Not Dim Charm of Mrs. Nellie Tayloe Ross." June 7, 1953, 1.

Jackson, W. Turrentine. "The Governorship of Wyoming, 1885–1889: A Study in Territorial Politics." *Pacific Historical Review* 13, no. 1 (March 1944): 1–11.

Junge, Mark. J.E. *Stimson, Photographer of the West*. Norman: University of Nebraska Press, 1985.

*Kansas City Times*. "In the Tradition of Hamilton, Group Is Testing U.S. Coins." February 12, 1953, 12.

Kassel, Michael E. "Thunder on High: Cheyenne, Denver and Aviation Supremacy on the Rocky Mountain Front Range." Master's thesis, University of Wyoming, 2007.

*Lakeview Cemetery Living History Walk*. Cheyenne, WY: Cheyenne Genealogical and Historical Society, August 20, 2022. Pamphlet.

*Lakeview Cemetery Tour*. Cheyenne: Wyoming Council for the Humanities, Wyoming Centennial Commission and the City of Cheyenne, 1990. Pamphlet.

*Laramie Boomerang.* "Details of Murder of Willie Nickel." July 21, 1901.

Laramie County Chapter, Wyoming State Historical Society. *Cheyenne Landmarks.* Cheyenne, WY: Pioneer Printing, 1976.

*Laramie Republican.* "The Richardson Funeral at Cheyenne Today." August 20, 1912, 5.

Larson, T.A. *History of Wyoming.* Lincoln: University of Nebraska Press, 1963.

Lightner, Sam, Jr. *Wyoming: A History of the American West.* Lander, WY: Summits and Crux Publishing, 2020.

Lyon, Dan. J. *The Girl Guards of Wyoming.* Charleston, SC: The History Press, 2019.

Mackey, Mike. "Nellie Tayloe Ross and Wyoming Politics." *Journal of the West* 42, no. 3 (Summer 2003): 25–31, 33.

Massie, Michael A. "Reform Is Where You Find It: The Roots of Woman Suffrage in Wyoming." *Annals of Wyoming* 62, no. 1 (Spring 1990): 2–22.

McCreery, Lucia. "The Roughest Mountains and Deepest Canons: William Richards and the Boundary Survey of 1874." www.WyoHistory.org.

Mead, Elwood. Water Education Foundation.

Mill, Kim. Personal interview with the author, Starley Talbott. November 10, 2022.

Moulton, Candy, and Flossie Moulton. *Steamboat, Legendary Bucking Horse.* Glendo, WY: High Plains Press, 1992.

Newman, Deidre. Email correspondence with author Starley Talbott. November 1–12, 2022.

*Northern Wyoming Herald.* "E.T. Payton Suspected." October 13, 1911, 1.

O'Hashi, Alan. *Beyond Heart Mountain.* North Hampton, NH: Winter Goose Publishing, 2022.

*Omaha Daily Bee.* "Weddings and Engagements." September 14, 1902, 6.

O'Neal, Bill. *Cheyenne: A Biography of the "Magic City" of the Plains.* Austin, TX: Eakin Press, 2006.

*Paducah Sun.* "Nellie Tayloe Ross, First Woman Governor, Nears 100." November 11, 1976, 1.

*Platte Valley Lyre.* "Chatterton-Wyland." October 25, 1900, 9.

———. "County Ticket." September 28, 1888, 8.

———. "Rawlins Drug Store," March 7, 1889, 4.

Qualls, Paula. Personal interview with the author Starley Talbott. August 19, 2022.

*Rawlins Republican.* "Convention Proceedings." September 27, 1894, 1.

———. "Republican Convention Met in Casper." August 8, 1894, 8.

———. "The State Legislature." November 20, 1890, 4.

———. "William A. Richards, Republican Nominee for Governor." August 16, 1894, 1.

———. "Wyoming's Next Governor." August 9, 1894, 8.

*Rawlins Semi-Weekly Republican.* "Wyoming Southern." July 29, 1899, 1.

Rea, Tom. "The Ambition of Nellie Tayloe Ross." www.WyoHistory.org.

———. "Booze, Cops, and Bootleggers: Enforcing Prohibition in Central Wyoming." www.WyoHistory.org.

Richards, W.A. "William A. Richards Family Papers, 1870–1965." Archives West.

Riske, Milt. *Cheyenne Frontier Days: A Marker from Which to Reckon All Events.* Cheyenne, WY: Frontier Printing Inc., 1984.

Roberts, Phil. "The Fetterman Hospital Association: Cooperative Health Care on the Range in the 1880s." *Magazine of Western History* 44, no. 3 (Summer 1994): 63–69.

———. "Law and Lawyers in Territorial Wyoming: An Overview." *Wyoming Almanac.*

Ross, Nellie Tayloe Papers: 1880–1998. Archives West.

*Saratoga Sun.* "Absorption of the Southern," August 10, 1899, 1.

———. "News from the Western Region." July 13, 1899, 2.

Scheer, Teva J. *Governor Lady: The Life and Times of Nellie Tayloe Ross.* Columbia: University of Missouri Press, 2005.

*Selma Times and Messenger.* "Valuable Plantation for Sale at Public Auction." February 11, 1868, 2.

*Sheridan Post.* "Colorado River Commission Meets." January 8, 1922, 1.

———. "Engineer Inspecting Irrigation Projects." August 16, 1919, 4.

Talbott, Starley. *Platte County.* Charleston, SC: Arcadia Publishing, 2009.

Talbott, Starley, and Linda Graves Fabian. *Cheyenne Frontier Days.* Charleston, SC: Arcadia Publishing, 2013.

———. *A History of the Wyoming Capitol.* Charleston, SC: The History Press, 2019.

Talbott, Starley, and Michael E. Kassel. *A History Lover's Guide to Cheyenne.* Charleston, SC: The History Press, 2021.

———. *Wyoming Airmail Pioneers.* Charleston, SC: The History Press, 2017.

———. *Wyoming's Friendly Skies.* Charleston, SC: The History Press, 2020.

Taylor, Paula Bauman. *F.E. Warren Air Force Base.* Charleston, SC: Arcadia Publishing, 2012.

Vandehei, Steve. Email correspondence with author Starley Talbott. May 13–20, 2021.

Van Pelt, Lori. "Bill Carlisle, Gentleman Bandit." www.WyoHistory.org.

———. *Capital Characters of Old Cheyenne*. Glendo, WY: High Plains Press, 2006.

———. "Cheyenne, Magic City of the Plains." October 30, 2017. www.WyoHistory.org.

———. "Eisenhower's 1919 Road Trip and the Interstate Highway System." www.WyoHist.org.

Weidel, Nancy. *Cheyenne: 1867–1917*. Charleston, SC: Arcadia Publishing, 2009.

Williams, George. "C.B. Irwin: High Roller." *Persimmon Hill* 7, no. 2 (1977): 18–25.

*Wyoming Industrial Journal*. "Governor Richards' Address." August 1, 1901, 19.

*Wyoming Press*. "Frank C. Emerson." July 17, 1926, 1.

———. "Gov. Richards Funeral Impressive." August 24, 1912, 8.

———. "Neighboring Claimants." July 8, 1926, 7.

———. "State Must Be Protected by Water Treaty." April 8, 1922, 4.

*Wyoming Semi-Weekly Tribune*. "Old Steamboat, World's Worst Bucking Broncho, Is Mercifully Shot." October 16, 1914, 1.

———. "Red Cross Issues Appeal for Aid." January 12, 1909, 6.

———. "Small Majorities." November 25, 1904, 1.

———. "Stoll Is Defeated." November 15, 1904, 6.

———. "Why Dr. Barber Will Be Missed." May 25, 1915, 4.

*Wyoming State Journal*. "Emerson Declares the Principles of His Candidacy." July 14, 1926, 1.

*Wyoming State Tribune*. "Aged Lady Dies, Mrs. Lucy Phillips, Aged 106." May 8, 1910.

———. "Anti-Gambling Law Is Valid." February 18, 1904, 5.

———. "Colonel Roosevelt Urges Election Robert D. Carey as Wyoming Governor." October 18, 1918, 1.

———. "Colorado River Is Give and Take Matter, Emerson," April 12, 1922, 5.

———. "Commend Scott's Decision." September 11, 1905, 8.

———. "Dr. Amos W. Barber, Who Was Youngest Governor of Wyoming, Is Called." May 19, 1915, 1.

———. "Election Cases," May 9, 1905, 4.

———. "Gambling Houses Close." September 20, 1905, 1.

———. "Gov. Carey and Cabinet are Sworn In." January 6, 1919, 1.

———. "Governor Ross Seriously Ill; Operated Upon." September 25, 1924, 1.

———. "John Gordon Tells of Great Service of Carey to Wyoming." February 1, 1924, 9.

———. "Joseph M. Carey, Grand Old Man of Wyoming, Succumbs to Sickness of Long Duration." February 6, 1924, 1.

———. "Leaders Set Good Example for Laymen." October 26, 1918, 4.

———. "Republican Victories in State and Nation." November 6, 1918, 1.

———. "Return from Australia." July 17, 1912, 8.

———. "Richards in Australia and Will Stay There for Some Time." July 7, 1912, 8.

———. "Rides Up Capitol Steps with Ultimatum." July 9, 1919, 8.

———. "Ross Elected." September 1, 1905, 5.

———. "Ross, Gov. William B. Tributes to Joseph M. Carey at Capitol Memorial Service." February 17, 1924, 4.

———. "School Fund Law Carries: Severance Tax Apparently Has Failed to Pass." November 9, 1924, 8.

———. "Severance Tax Urged by Ross." July 30, 1924, 5.

———. "Solons Made Record Time in Enactment of Ratifying Measure." January 16, 1919, 8.

———. "To Enforce State Anti-Gambling Law." September 19, 1905, 1.

———. "W.A. Richards Shows Where Leader Lies Again." July 15, 1912, 1.

———. "W.R. Stoll Is Still Prosecuting Attorney." January 6, 1905, 8.

———. "Wyoming' s Water." April 9, 1922, 4.

*Wyoming State Tribune, SunDAY Magazine.* "The Last of the West." July 24, 1977, 8.

*Wyoming Tribune.* "Governor's Four Years Sufficient, Says Carey." January 4, 1915, 1.

———. "The Governor's Tribute." September 28, 1899, 4.

———. "Indians, Cowboys and Vast Number of Wyoming People Pay Last Honors to Rider." July 23, 1917, 1.

*Wyoming Tribune, Stockman Farmer.* "Horrible Tragedy at Ex-Gov. Richards' Ranch." 1911, 2.

## Websites

American Heritage Center. www.uwyo.edu/ahe.

Cheyenne Botanic Gardens. www.botanic.org.

Cheyenne Frontier Days™ Old West Museum. www.oldwestmuseum.org.

Cheyenne Genealogical and Historical Society. www.cghswyoming.org.

Cheyenne Street Railway Trolley. www.cheyennetrolley.com.

Cowgirls of the West. www.cowgirlsofthewestmuseum.com.

Find a Grave. www.findagrave.com.

History.net. www.historynet.com.

Lakeview Cemetery. www.cheyennecity.org.

Nelson Museum of the West. www.nelsonmuseum.org.

Visit Cheyenne. www.cheyenne.org.

Water Education Foundation. www.watereducation.org.

WyoHistory.org: A Project of the Wyoming State Historical Society. www.wyohistory.org.

Wyoming Governors, State of Wyoming website. www.wyo.gov.

Wyoming National Guard Museum. www.wyngm.wyo.gov.

Wyoming Newspapers: From the Wyoming State Library. www.newspapers.wyo.gov.

Wyoming State Archives. www.wyoarchives.state.wyo.us.

Wyoming State Historic Preservation Office. www.wyoshpo.state.wyo.us.

# ABOUT THE AUTHORS

Starley Talbott has been a freelance author for more than fifty years. She has been published in numerous newspapers and magazines throughout the Rocky Mountain region and is the author of ten books, including three Arcadia Publishing titles, *Platte County*, *Fort Laramie* and *Cheyenne Frontier Days*, and three History Press titles, *Wyoming Airmail Pioneers: A History of the Wyoming Capitol*, *Wyoming's Friendly Skies* and *A History Lover's Guide to Cheyenne*. Starley holds a bachelor's degree from the University of Wyoming and a master's degree from the University of Nevada. She has lived in several states and foreign countries, loves to travel and has a deep appreciation for history. She is a member of Wyoming Writers, the Platte County Historical Society and the Wyoming State Historical Society.

Michael E. Kassel serves as the curator of collections and the associate director of operations at the Cheyenne Frontier Days Old West Museum. He is an adjunct professor of history at Laramie County Community College in Cheyenne, Wyoming. He holds a bachelor's degree in historic preservation from Southeast Missouri State University, an associate of the arts degree in history from Laramie County Community College and a master of arts degree from the University of Wyoming. He is the author of *Thunder on High: Cheyenne, Denver and Aviation Supremacy on the Rocky Mountain Front Range* and *The United Air Lines Stewardess School in Cheyenne, Wyoming*. He is the coauthor of *Wyoming Air Mail Pioneers*, *Wyoming's Friendly Skies* and *A History Lover's Guide to Cheyenne* from The History Press.

*Visit us at*
www.historypress.com

Printed in the USA
CPSIA information can be obtained
at www.ICGtesting.com
LVHW080828011123
762598LV00003B/3